What people are saying about

Sexual Dynamics in the Circle

I was so pleased to get a preview copy of *Sexual Dynamics in the Circle: Magic, Man & Woman* to read; a good, proper book on sex magic is long overdue and this one is seriously refreshing. Mélusine Draco's approach is very down to earth and, at the same time, fully with spirit. Gone are the crazy, titillating, salacious styles of far too many other books on the subject, Draco shows you and explains what actually happens and helps you understand this for yourself. In *Sexual Dynamics in the Circle*, we learn about working with the two principles of the universe that we know, here on Earth, as gender, female and male, the duality that is all creation from forming stars on down. And we're able to get away from extreme feminism too, always a good thing; the powers of goddess and god are twined and combined, they don't battle for supremacy. If you want to learn more about how the genders combine to work magic this is the book to read.
Elen Sentier, Shaman and author

Pagan Portals

Sexual Dynamics
in the Circle

Magic, Man & Woman

Pagan Portals
Sexual Dynamics
in the Circle

Magic, Man & Woman

Mélusine Draco

MOON
BOOKS

Winchester, UK
Washington, USA

JOHN HUNT PUBLISHING

First published by Moon Books, 2021
Moon Books is an imprint of John Hunt Publishing Ltd., No. 3 East Street, Alresford
Hampshire SO24 9EE, UK
office@jhpbooks.net
www.johnhuntpublishing.com
www.moon-books.net

For distributor details and how to order please visit the 'Ordering' section on our website.

Text copyright: Mélusine Draco 2020

ISBN: 978 1 78904 589 5
978 1 78904 590 1 (ebook)
Library of Congress Control Number: 2020933107

A CIP catalogue record for this book is available from the British Library.

Design: Stuart Davies

UK: Printed and bound by CPI Group (UK) Ltd, Croydon, CR0 4YY
Printed in North America by CPI GPS partners

We operate a distinctive and ethical publishing philosophy in all areas of our business, from our global network of authors to production and worldwide distribution.

Contents

To the beloved company of the stars, the moon, and the sun;
to ocean, air, and the silence of space;
to jungle glacier, and desert,
soft earth, clear water, and fire on my heart,
To a certain waterfall in a high forest;
to night rain upon the roof and the wide leaves,
grass in the wind, tumult of sparrows in a bush,
and eyes which give light to the day.
[Alan Watts, *Nature, Man & Woman*]

In the Beginning ...

One of the most significant social changes in the 20th-century was the wedge driven between the men and women of Craft as a result of negative social media and political feminism. From a purely magical perspective the battle of the sexes has possibly been one of the most negative crusades in the history of humankind since everything in the entire Universe is made up from a balance or harmony of opposing energies. Men and women *are* as different as night to day but they still part of the same ancient *homo sapiens* coin – regardless of their individual sexuality and diversity.

If we wish to explore magic and mysticism on a wider scale, however, we must learn to look beyond gender politics and prejudices, and accept the opposite sex *because* of the differences and similarities that are all part of the equilibrium of magic in all its forty shades of grey. Spirituality is, in itself, genderless and those with an uncompromising chauvinistic or feminist outlook should carry out a considerable amount of soul-searching with regard to magical practice because none of us can afford to be blinkered by prejudice or hampered by refusing to accept another witch or magus on the grounds of gender incompatibility alone.

Pan and Hecate are *not* irreconcilable. Both are night-wanderers who put the fear of the gods up unsuspecting travellers who find themselves abroad during the hours of darkness. Although demanding profound respect, neither belonged to the pantheon of Olympus but were too powerful to be ignored by the later compilers of Greek mythos; because both are ancient deities from a primordial Old Europe strata of myth that the Greeks found difficult to reconcile with their Olympian genealogy. The ancient mainstream Greek religion, with which we are most familiar, appears to have developed out of the in-coming Indo-European faiths and although very little is known about the earliest periods there are suggestive hints that some local elements go back even further than the Bronze Age to the agrarian culture of Neolithic Greece.

Both Pan and Hecate appear to have been particularly associated as being 'between the worlds' – being neither/nor when it came to tracing the fons et origo - or source and origin – of such potent entities. And as such they can be characterized as liminal beings that bridge the primordial, medieval and modern worlds: Hecate as the triple goddess of the moon and witchcraft, while Pan identified with the alleged 'devil' of the witches and the Horned God. And of course, the moon goddess was seduced by Pan, who gave her the gift of a white horse or, alternately, a pair of white oxen. Virgil briefly describes how the god Pan seduced her by luring her down from the sky with a shining lamb's fleece. The story may also be connected with the birth of the goddess of youth, Pandeia, whose name-prefix naturally suggests the god.

> *Twas with gift of such snowy wool, if we may trust the tale, that Pan, Arcadia's god, charmed and beguiled you, O Luna (the Moon-Selene), calling you to the depths of the woods; nor did you scorn his call.* [Theoi.com]

Whether the pagan community likes to admit it or not – there are now *two* distinct approaches to contemporary witchcraft. One is the cleaned up, politically correct, socially acceptable form of neo-goddess worship that hails deity as an insipid medieval Madonna-like creature; an amalgam of the Virgin Mary/Diana/Gaia/Isis representing the maiden/mother/grandma and totally disrespecting the true image of the crone/destroyer. There is often little or no mention of the second aspect, since the god's image is more difficult to render impotent – it is incongruous to depict the Horned God skipping around like Basil Fotherington-Tomas chanting *'Hello birds, hello trees, hello clouds, hello sky'* and therefore his image is suppressed even by many males of the neo-pagan species.

Unfortunately, the former is increasingly becoming the generalised public face of witchcraft because traditionalists from pre-repeal of the Witchcraft Act traditions, who prefer not to sanitize their male deity, have retreated back into the shadows through sheer exasperation at the trivialisation of their beliefs. The traditional Old Craft approach to deity acknowledges the dual importance of both male *and* female elements which is essential to effective magical working. There are few apologists among the ranks of the traditionalists since their uncompromising attitude is governed by certainty: they know who they are and what is expected of them despite contemporary thought blaming elitism, hierarchy and patriarchal influences for all that is wrong with 21st-century witchcraft.

As a result, traditional Crafters appear less and less frequently on television and, more often than not, decline to give interviews for the national press decked out in flowing robes with garlands of flowers, or waving a sword around. Neither do the traditionalists have any problems with the identity of their deity since there is only one Creator, and the male/female/androgynous images merely differing facets of the One. This One, however, often presents a darker, less benign countenance than its modern-day adherents would like to admit – and it is towards these images of traditional Craft that neo-paganism points an accusing finger of being practitioners of dubious sexual rites – both in the past, and in the here and now. Is it any wonder that the 'Perfect Love and Perfect Trust' philosophy of neo-paganism cannot be reconciled with the 'Trust None' approach of traditional British Old Craft?

The occult revival of the 1970s, which began as an intelligent, almost scientific investigation of the supernatural, now appears to have taken second place to a rebirth of superstition. Today's eclectic shop-a-rounder wants sound-bites and scrappy bits of information that enables them to pass themselves off as knowledgeable members of the pagan community. There is also a growing concern about the dumbed-down versions of magical/mystical applications that appear to be among the most popular reading material now available which, to quote Dion Fortune, isn't paganism but decomposing Christianity:

> *The popularising of esoteric ideas and methodology has enabled people – who are not really ready to make the self-transformations demanded of initiates – to adopt an occult persona and salve their anxieties by relying on occult junk. Serious occultism isn't for everyone ... and so, particularly in the past decades, there has been a significant increase in people who rely on superstition, and who lack discernment. The same result is reached in paganism by another form of superstition: that of an unquestioning belief in paganism as a religion per se. Recently, far too many people have adopted paganism as a belief far too quickly instead of developing a discernment and appreciation of the difference between paganism and orthodox religion. They have brought their Old Aeon religious superstitious baggage with them, only to clutter up and confuse the development of paganism – as well as themselves.* [What You Call Time]

And just as there is no original thought in Christian doctrine – since what they have was culled from nearly every religious culture they suppressed along the way – so today's paganism is doing the same with its eclectic coupling of loosely-bound ideas and self-promotion. The problems this causes on a higher magical level (as in many other departments of occult science) lies outside the scope of the average witchlet; resulting in the popular gender-specific, eclectic 'pick and mix' approach to magical practice that has emerged out of its unconditional implementation. In Old Craft the power of the god is still honoured as a balancing element between himself and the goddess – and long may they reign!

Sex magic can be divided into two types: folk magic and metaphysical magic. The first and most popular being the unusual and commonly used procedures of witchcraft including rites, incantatory spells and food preparation that make it possible to combat unrequited love, cure male impotence or determine the sex of an unborn child. The second, higher and often considered 'elitist' type of magic consists of taking control of the practitioner's own sexuality and directing it in a way that brings about the full magnitude of their personality. In this domain we find the ascetics who use sex to obtain enlightenment and sacred trance, increase their psychic powers, and have an effect on the invisible world.

Sexual magic's sphere of operation – limited since the Middle Ages to rare translations of the Qabalah and esoteric Christianity – was expanded over the 20th-century with information flooding in from the East. Up until that time in the West, it was still believed that magical forces were dark powers governed by demons. It was subsequently learned that these were luminous forces that determined experiences of the divine and drew the best possible advantage from the energy centres of the human body ...

Mélusine Draco
Glen of Aherlow - 2020

Chapter One

Old Lasses and Lads

Come, lasses and lads,
Take leave of your dads,
And away to the may-pole hie;
For every he has got him a she,
And the minstrel's standing by;
-The Maypole – traditional English folk ballad

Time and culture have divided and modified belief into many species and countless varieties. Nevertheless, however much the imagination was allowed to tinker with it, the governing spirit of that belief was sexuality – the worship of the generative (fertility) principle of man and Nature, male and female. Rites and adoration were sometimes paid to the male, sometimes to the female, or to the two in one ...

Professor Richard Kieckhefer [*Magic in the Middle Ages*], however, gives a powerful insight into the influence that classical literature had on the insidious viewpoint of scholastic minds responsible for witchcraft persecution manuals and sexual heresy. Many fictional works such as those by Homer and Vigil were cited as historical *fact*, and the legendary Circe became a flesh and blood example of personified evil in women. Classical literature, with which the educated of the time would have been familiar, contains numerous instances of magical potions and spells used by women to avenge themselves on a jilting lover, an unfaithful husband, or a hated rival. Seneca, Theocritus, Lucan, Horace and many others provided the basic witch-hunt material for the persecutors and in Kieckhefer's own words: *'If medieval Europeans has known no other sources for misogyny, they could easily have learned it from these texts'.*

The mythology of archaic gods and goddesses is not merely a collection of colourful stories but a window on the ancient civilisations, their thoughts and values, and an insight into the way our forebears viewed their deities. Ancient mythologies frequently represented the divine as deities with human forms and qualities; resembling human beings not only in appearance and personality. Greek deities such as Zeus and Apollo were depicted in human form exhibiting both commendable and despicable human traits: anthropomorphism in this case is, more specifically, 'anthropotheism' as these two roared and pounced their way the length and breadth of pre-Hellenic Greece, up-ending many an unsuspecting maiden or nymph in the verdant undergrowth. [*Greek Myths*]

Legend has it that the most beautiful statue in the ancient world was carved in marble by a celebrated sculptor named Praxiteles. Aphrodite at Knidos (in ancient Asia Minor, or modern-day Turkey) is long since lost – today we have only later copies and guesswork to help us imagine what she would have looked like. She would certainly have been naked, probably holding a robe as though disturbed as she gets out of a bath. The likeness was deemed so uncanny that one Greek author wrote an epigram, attributed to the goddess, in which she asks: '*Where did Praxiteles see me naked?*' She was so beautiful that a man fell in love with her, and spent the night locked in her temple; his passion drove him mad, and he threw himself from the nearby cliffs the next day. But, for all her divine powers, this particular Aphrodite was modeled on a 4th century BC prostitute, named Phryne ... and though Phryne was surely a very beautiful woman, her name literally means 'toad'!

The Greeks had a mania for male public nudity, something they shared with no other ancient society. Non-Greeks considered it most peculiar - and men in Greek art are often shown nude. They would exercise naked, and managed to avoid sunburn by covering themselves with oil and dust, using it as an elementary sun-block, which they would scrape off at the end of the exercise session with a *strigil*. In ancient Greece the rules of beauty were all important. Things were good for men who were buff and glossy. And for women, fuller-figured redheads were in favour - but they had to contend with an ominous undercurrent, as historian Bettany Hughes explains:

> *A full-lipped, cheek-chiselled man in Ancient Greece knew two things - that his beauty was a blessing (a gift of the gods no less) and that his perfect exterior hid an inner perfection. For the Greeks a beautiful body was considered direct evidence of a beautiful mind. They even had a word for it - kaloskagathos - which meant being gorgeous to look at, and hence being a good person. Not very politically correct, I know, but the horrible truth is that pretty Greek boys would have swaggered around convinced they were triply blessed - beautiful, brainy and god-beloved. For years, classical Greek sculpture was believed to be a perfectionist fantasy - an impossible ideal, but we now think a number of the exquisite statues from the 5th to the 3rd Centuries BC were in fact cast from life - a real person was covered with plaster, and the mould created was then used to make the sculpture.*

The Apollo Belvedere is a Roman copy of an ancient Greek bronze statue. It is unknown who sculpted the current version but Leochares may have sculpted the original in the 4th century BC. The Apollo Belvedere has for a long time been considered as the ideal depiction of male beauty and antiquarian Johann Winckelmann writes of it: *'His build is sublimely superhuman, and his stance bears witness to the fullness of his grandeur'*. Along with similar ancient Greek statues of warrior-athletes, the Doryphoros, or 'Spear-Bearer', established a standard of male beauty that abides today in the West: a muscular, athletic mesomorph!

There have been many ideas over time and across different

cultures of what the feminine beauty 'ideal' is for a woman's body image. How well a woman followed these beauty ideals could also influence her social status within her culture. The idealized women of artists like Raphael were routinely curvy, pale but with slightly flushed cheeks, and soft, round faces. Raphael admitted that most of his paintings were not based on real models, simply his imaginings of what a beautiful woman would look like. Artists continued to portray the 'ideal' woman as curvy and voluptuous all the way through to the 17th and 18th centuries. The Flemish painter Peter Paul Rubens was even the namesake of the term 'rubenesque', meaning plump or rounded, as he often depicted women with sensuous curves.

Regardless of the perceived physical attractiveness of men and women, however, sexual morality and ethics can only be viewed in the light of the laws, customs and fashion of the times. During the Middle Ages there was a deep entrenchment of an alternative morality to that required by the clergy, which Jeffrey Richards (*Sex, Dissidence and Damnation*) identifies as *'a morality of pre-Christian tribal and peasant society'*, in which sexual life was unrestricted by religious dogma. *'Marriages of the time were often informal affairs and easily dissolved; and if the sexual act was believed to be innocent and pleasure derived from it, then this was not disagreeable to God.'* Needless to say, these pagan attitudes were anathema to the early Church fathers who associated all illicit sex with the Devil and subsequently there were certain elements in paganism that defied Christian absorption, particularly the fertility cults.

To compound the evil, the authors of the *Malleus Maleficarum* claimed that all witchcraft came from carnal lust *'which is in women insatiable'* and *'all wickedness is but little to the wickedness of a woman'*. In view of this ecclesiastical misogyny, it is not surprising that medieval women clung firmly to their pagan faith which placed male and female at level pegging. The Church, however, knew how to threaten a man's masculinity and held over him the constant risk of a wife, daughter, sister or mother succumbing to carnal temptation with demons; every female member of his family was a potential danger to his manhood. According to Alan Watts, this association of sexuality with the sacred conjured up the most superstitious fears and fantasies, including the suspicion that it must have something to do with Satanism and the weird practices of black magic and the left-hand path!

Although it has long been accepted as 'gospel' that there is not one grain of truth in the *Malleus Maleficarum*, this perverted brainchild of two deviant Dominicans, became the irrefutable Papal textbook of torture and murder through medieval Europe. Professor Richards defines it as a work of *'pathological misogynism and sex-obsession'*. The witch-trials took common, everyday occurrences and magnified them out of all proportion to illustrate the manner in which the Devil's disciples served him. St Augustine had been banging on *ad nauseam* about the sins of the flesh and so chastity became *the* Christian virtue.

All of which went against the grain for the average man and woman who had a normal pagan appetite for fornication. Controversial German theologian, Uta Ranke-Heinemann in *Eunuchs for the Kingdom of Heaven*, maintains that the church fathers were asexual who de-sexed themselves and then set about de-sexing the rest of humanity, with Augustine piling on the agony by declaring that even marriage consummated for pleasure's sake was a mortal sin – the act of fornication would consign the participants into the fires of Hell! The late Michael Howard, esoteric author and editor of *The Cauldron*, summed it all up by saying:

> ... *this aspect of the feminine has always been rejected by patriarchal cultures whose sexual puritanism transformed it into a demonic symbol because they were incapable of handling the potent erotic energies associated with it.*

A bold pagan rebellion first manifested in the United Kingdom in the 1950s, with individuals like Charles Cardell and Gerald Gardner popularizing their nature-based beliefs. By the 1960's and throughout the 1970's multiple variations of more structured applications began sprouting up within the USA, with Wicca being the most well-known of the neo-pagan movements. Cardell, Gardner's rival during the 1950's in England, is alleged to be the one who actually coined the term 'Wiccans' after playing around with the Anglo-Saxon etymology. Wicca was introduced to North America in 1964 by Raymond Buckland, an expatriate Briton who visited Gardner's Isle of Man coven to gain initiation. Interest in the USA spread quickly, and while many were initiated, many more non-initiates compiled their own rituals based on published sources or their own fancy.

Men were not the only founders of pagan beliefs. Another significant development was the creation by feminists in the late 1960's and 1970's of an eclectic movement known as Dianic Wicca, or Dianic Witchcraft. The 'Grand Dames' of modern witchcraft, however, such as Patricia Crowther, Doreen Valiente, Sybil Leek and Monique Wilson all worked with male associates and obviously didn't feel the need to espouse magical/political feminism.

Much of the criticism that has been leveled at witchcraft in general and Wicca in particular is its penchant for nude ceremonies, or working 'sky-clad'. If the truth be told, a lot of the allegations stems from Gerald Gardner's personal adherence to nudism, which he introduced into his Craft workings. And for those *News-of-the-World* type photographs that are still regularly trotted out to demonstrate how risqué Craft was back in the day. In the forty years this author has been involved with the occult fraternity I have only ever been invited to participate in one nude ritual – which was deferred due to inclement weather!

Ritual nudity is no different to stripping off while on holiday in the south of France and rather than having any sexual overtones is rather a somber and staid affair. This was all well and good when we were young and vigorous … but with the passing of the years we all succumb to the gravitational pull of age and aging. Visualize for a moment folds of loose, bare flesh cavorting around the Circle to the strains of *The Lincolnshire Poacher* and it should be blatantly obvious that there is nothing erotic about sky-clad group working and we can almost hear those age-less gods howling with derisive laughter at the spectacle!

The earliest known *practical* teachings of sex magic in the West come from 19th-century African-American medical doctor, occultist, spiritualist, trance medium, and writer, Paschal Beverly Randolph, under the heading of *The Mysteries of Eulis*:

If a man has an intelligent and loving wife, with whom he is in complete accord, he can work out the problems [of how to achieve magical results] by her aid. They are a radical soul-sexive series of energies...The rite is a prayer in all cases, and the most powerful [that] earthly beings can employ...it is best for both man and wife to act together for the attainment of the mysterious objects sought.

Success in any case requires the adjuvancy of a superior woman. THIS IS THE LAW! A harlot or low woman is useless for all such lofty and holy purposes, and just so is a bad, impure, passion-driven apology for a man. The woman shall not be one who accepts rewards for compliance; nor a virgin; or under eighteen years of age; or another's wife; yet must be one who hath known man and who has been and still is capable of intense mental, volitional and affectional energy, combined with perfect sexive and orgasmal ability; for it requires a double crisis to succeed...

The entire mystery can be given in very few words, and they are: An upper room; absolute personal, mental, and moral cleanliness both of the man and wife. An observance of the law just cited during the entire term of the experiment - 49 days. Formulate the desire and keep it in mind during the whole period and especially when making the nuptive prayer, during which no word may be spoken, but the thing desired be strongly thought...

From his experiences in England, France, Egypt and the Turkish Empire during the 1850s and 1860s, Randolph took back to America a system of occult beliefs and practices (i.e. magic mirror, hashish use and sexual magic) that revolutionized magical practice in the USA, although as can be determined from the extract quoted above, prudery remained the order of the day. The systems of magic he taught left their traces on many subsequent occultists, including Madame Blavatsky and her Theosophical Society, and are still practiced today by several occult organizations in Europe and American that carry on his work. In addition to his work as a trance medium, Randolph trained as a doctor of medicine, writing and publishing both fictional and instructive books based on his theories of health, sexuality, spiritualism and occultism.

Having long used the pseudonym 'The Rosicrucian' for his spiritualist and occult writings, Randolph eventually founded the *Fraternitas Rosae Crucis* in 1858: their first lodge in San Francisco inaugurated in 1861, is the oldest Rosicrucian organization in the United States, which dates back to the era of the American Civil War. This group, still in existence, today avoids mention of Randolph's interest in sex magic, but his magico-sexual theories and techniques formed the basis of much of the teachings of other occult fraternities. *Paschal Beverly Randolph: A Nineteenth-Century Black American Spiritualist, Rosicrucian, and Sex Magician* by John Patrick Deveney is the first scholarly work on Randolph and includes the full text of his two most important manuscript works on sexual magic.

In the latter part of the 19th century, sexual reformer Ida Craddock published several works dealing with sacred sexuality, most notably *Heavenly Bridegrooms* and *Psychic Wedlock*. Aleister Crowley reviewed the former in *The Equinox*, stating that it was:

'one of the most remarkable human documents ever produced'. He goes on to say:

> I am very far from agreeing with all that this most talented woman sets forth in her paper, but she certainly obtained initiated knowledge of extraordinary depth. She seems to have had access to certain most concealed sanctuaries ... She has put down statements in plain English which are positively staggering. This book is of incalculable value to every student of occult matters. No Magick library is complete without it.

As academic Vere Chappell comments, this is quite an endorsement from Crowley, and perhaps even more significant in that he signed the review 'Baphomet', using his magical name as Tenth Degree of the famous *Ordo Templi Orientis.*

The paper entitled *Psychic Wedlock* was of particular interest to the OTO, as it describes a three-degree system of initiation by sexual means. The first degree, which Ida dubs 'Alphaism', calls for the development of self-control. In particular, *'sex union is forbidden, except for the express purpose of creating a child'*. In the second degree, called 'Dianism', *'sex union is enjoined in absolute self-control and aspiration to the highest'*. This is accomplished in two phases: first, by learning to delay ejaculation and prolong the union indefinitely; and second, after mastering the first phase, acquiring the ability to go through the ecstasy of orgasm without ejaculation. She describes similar practices of self-control on the part of the female as well. Finally, the third degree inculcates *'communion with Deity as the third partner in marital union'*. This degree also has two phases: the first is to fulfill the duty to aspire to communion with the 'Great Thinker' during sexual ecstasy; and the second is to attain the state of joy which accrues to both the 'Great Thinker' and to the partner's through such communion. Reminiscent of the lines *'I am above you and in you. My ecstasy is in yours. My joy is to see your joy.'* from the *Book of the Law.*

In 1893 Ida Craddock fell foul of a man named Anthony Comstock, founder of a self-ordained moral police squad called The Society for the Suppression of Vice, who pursued a vendetta against her that eventually led to her suicide in 1902 rather than go to prison.

In her massive study of religious sexuality entitled Lunar & Sex Worship, Ida argued that 'the moon was a more ancient deity than the sun, and that she was therefore recognized as the superior of the sun-god, who, as being the exponent of a later religion, could triumph only after receiving her sanction'. This theory resembles remarkably Crowley's description of the Aeons of Isis and Osiris. Her development of the argument cites a tremendous range of sources, including Assyrian, Babylonian, Hindu, Irish, Greek, Norse, Jewish, Christian, Islamic, Chinese, Egyptian, African, but to name a few. [Book of Lies: The Disinformation Guide to Magick and the Occult]

Born in Philadelphia in 1857, Ida Craddock became involved in occultism around the age of thirty. She attended classes at the Theosophical Society and began studying a tremendous amount of materials on various occult subjects. She began studying esoteric sexuality, combining her extensive knowledge of folklore and mythology with various occult sources, since during this period there was a growing trend of increased sexual awareness and open discourse of sexuality in society. Burton had brought back translations of the *Kama Sutra* and *Ananga Ranga* from India, and Havelock Ellis had begun applying scientific principles to the study of sexuality. This was the first sexual revolution, long before the 1960's, as the western world emerged from its Victorian prudery to start openly and objectively examining sex for the first time.

Sexual techniques from her *Psychic Wedlock* were later

reproduced in *Sex Magick* (1993) by OTO initiate Louis T Culling but '*although he does mention Craddock in his introduction he doesn't appear to give her the credit that she deserves for essentially providing him with the entire system*', comments Vere Chappell, who, in 2010 as Grand Treasurer General of the OTO published his biography *Sexual Outlaw, Erotic Mystic: The Essential Ida Craddock*. This is the most extensive collection of Craddock's work including original essays, diary excerpts, and suicide letters - one to her mother and one to the public.

When Winston Churchill called Russia '*a riddle wrapped in a mystery inside an enigma*', he could as well have been describing a daughter of Russia named Maria de Naglowska, says Donald C Traxler writing in *New Dawn Magazine*:

> *She was a poet, journalist, translator, author, occultist, and mystic (the latter perhaps most of all), but today few know anything about her. Those who have ever heard of her probably know her as the translator of P B Randolph's* Magia Sexualis *(which she did far more than translate). Others, who have shown more curiosity about her, will say that she was a Satanist (not true, though it is an impression that she fostered) and was the source of Randolph's subsequent influence in European magic. It has taken many years to get any reliable facts about her life, partly because she told different stories about herself. Her most important writings were published in very small editions (now almost impossible to get) and never translated into English. Consequently, this woman whose works should occupy a significant place in the history of Western religion, is now practically unknown, especially in English.*

Maria de Naglowska was born in St. Petersburg in 1883, the daughter of a prominent Czarist family. She went to the best schools, and got the best education that a young woman of the time could get. She was a linked with the Parisian surrealist movement and operated an occult society known as the *Confrérie de la Flèche d'or* (Brotherhood of the Golden Arrow) in Paris from 1932 to 1935. During these years she published a newsletter called *La Flèche* (*The Arrow*) that featured contributions from herself and other occultists while her own writings were considered so revolutionary that it earned her the name of *La Sophiale de Montparnasse* (The Wise Woman of Montparnasse). A small booklet (75 pages) of *Rituals of the Brotherhood of the Golden Arrow* are available in paperback – see http://newfleshpalladium. blogspot.com/

In 1932 she published a semi-autobiographical novella, *Le Rite sacré de l'amour magique* (*The Sacred Ritual of Magical Love*); followed by *La Lumière du sexe* (*The Light of Sex*), a mystic treatise and guide to sexual ritual that was required reading for those seeking to be initiated into the Brotherhood. Her later book on advanced sexual magic practices, *Le Mystère de la pendaison* (*The Hanging Mystery*) details her advanced teachings on the Third Term of the Trinity and the spiritually transformative power of sex; the practice of erotic ritual hanging, or autoerotic asphyxiation. Her explanation being that the latter helped the subject focus on their orgasm through sensory deprivation.

Naglowska also influenced the Surrealist art movement. The *Lexique succinct de l'érotisme* in the catalog of the 1959 International Surrealist Exhibition in Paris noted her important influence, while Surrealist Sarane Alexandrian wrote the only serious detailed account of her life - *Les Libérateurs de l'amour*. Julius Evola, in his book, *Eros and the Mysteries of Love: The Metaphysics of Sex* claimed that Naglowska often wrote for shock effect noting her '*deliberate intention to scandalize the reader through unnecessarily dwelling on Satanism*'. It may have been for such scandalous and provocative effect that she used Satanic rhetoric and imagery or it may have been for a more sophisticated symbolic illustration in her message that she referred to herself as '*a Satanic woman*'. She explicitly encouraged her disciples to imagine Satan as a force within humanity rather than as an external actual evil, destructive spirit; employing Satan as a symbol for man's desire for joy and freedom.

One ritual for which there exists a first-hand account recalls that the ceremony included a naked Naglowska lying supine upon the altar while a male initiate places a chalice upon her genitalia and proclaims:

> *I will strive by any means to illuminate myself, with the aid of a woman who knows how to love me with virgin love ... I will research with companions the initiatory erotic act, which, by transforming the heat into light arouses Lucifer from the satanic shades of masculinity.*

Donald Traxler is both a translator and student of the occult, and has recently finished a five-book series of the works of Maria de Naglowska, for Inner Traditions International: *Advanced Sex Magic: The Hanging Mystery Initiation; The Light of Sex: Initiation, Magic, and Sacrament; The Sacred Rite of Magical Love: A Ceremony of Word; Initiatic Eroticism and Other Occult Writings from La Flèche*; and *Flesh & Magia Sexualis: Sexual Practices for Magical Power* that are viewed as an important contribution to the literature of sex magic as developed in the 20th century. In addition, Marc Pluquet's *La Sophiale* is her biography, which as Maria's pupil, many believe that he was in the best position to write.

And not omitting the most sacred cow of the ritual magic fraternity, Dion Fortune, who published *The Philosophy of Love and Marriage* (1924) which was described as *'spiritualist eroticism'*. To meet her other world lovers, she made journeys in the astral plane using her own personal method that *'involved self-hypnosis achieved by means of a symbol. This symbol works like a door giving access to the invisible world'*. She therefore knew to what sector she was going, instead of wandering in search of adventure in the realm of intense erotic daydreaming:

These astral journeys are really lucid dreams in which one retains all one's faculties of choice, will-power and judgement. Mine always begin with a curtain of the symbolic colour through whose folds I pass. [Modern Ritual Magic]

As a member of the Golden Dawn she would have gained the requisite experience and competence, and in her novels and essays she developed 'a type of magic, called sex magic, even though it was a sexuality expressed in discreet terms' it is no less potent in its discretion.

Of course, no discussion on sex magic would be complete without mention of Aleister Crowley's Thelema - an occult philosophy/religion that embraces libertinism with a total disregard of authority or convention in sexual or religious matters. Sex magic (spelled sex *magick* in its Thelemic context) is any type of consensual sexual activity used in magical, ritualistic or otherwise religious and spiritual pursuits. One technique uses the energy of sexual arousal or orgasm with visualization of a desired result; the concept being that sexual energy is a potent force that can be harnessed to transcend any person's normally perceived reality

While the Ordo Templi Orientis included, from its inception, the teaching of sex magick in the highest degrees of the Order, when Crowley became head of the Order, he expanded on these teachings and integrated Thelema into the existing OTO system. Professor Hugh Urban, Professor of Comparative Religion at The Ohio State University, noted Crowley's emphasis on sex as *'the supreme magical power'* – while according to Crowley:

The Book of the Law solves the sexual problem completely. Each individual [both men and women] has an absolute right to satisfy his sexual instinct as is physiologically proper for him. The one injunction is to treat all such acts as sacraments. One should not eat as the brutes, but in order to enable one to do one's will. The same applies to sex. We must use every faculty to further the one object of our existence.

The Thelemic Handbook records that most of the accusations of misogyny and chauvinism come from those who have not developed an appreciation of his writing style ... or his humour. Many of his comments about women would be enough to raise the hackles of even the mildest-natured feminist should she decide to take his remarks out of context – which invariably happens. The type of woman he admired need to be 'wicked, independent, courageous, ambitious ...' and there wouldn't have been many of those on the hoof in Crowley's lifetime but the modern reader is often baffled by his (seemingly!) childish jokes and the serious things he had to say, and the playful way he said them.

It's true that he once commented that women should be delivered to the back door regularly, like the milk – but we've all heard worse from contemporary comedians – and Aleister Crowley was merely a product of his time. Neither could he ever be considered as a sexual predator in the manner of latter-day showbiz 'studs' whose antics regularly delighted the tabloid press. Today's politically-correct occultism also picks up on the 'fact' that Crowley hated women but in all of his writings there is little to support this alleged misogyny. There are plenty of sexist remarks but these were made at the turn of the century when attitudes were different and therefore cannot be taken out of context merely to make a point. To put things in perspective, Aleister Crowley hated *stupid* women, especially the mindless, prudish variety like his own mother, who hid behind a veil of respectable religiosity, whom he held (and with some justification) responsible for his own miserable and abusive childhood.

Nevertheless, magic, almost in its entirety, is connected to sexuality. It is through the natural magic of love that sex magic operates, harnessing the forces that join lovers together. In *The Great Work of the Flesh*, an extensive study of sex magic in the Eastern and Western Mystery Traditions, Sarane Alexandrian explains how there is a sex magic connected with every religion, spiritual belief system, and initiatory society. Exploring sexual practices in folk magic, high magic, alchemy, and religion, the author begins with a complete overview of love magic in the Middle Ages, including accounts of the use of potions, powders, spells, and enchantments, and reveals how these techniques related to the religious practices of the time. Providing complete practical information, he explains how, through sex magic, a couple can extract from each other what they are missing by way of virility and femininity, multiplying their energies tenfold and merging the carnal and spiritual worlds to *'experience transcendent adventures in the deepest depths of reality'*.

The persistent state of rivalry, opposition, or tension between males and females in today's society means that we don't acknowledge all the grey areas in life. The things we can't fit into a box. Life's paradoxes. Unknowns. The stuff that's difficult to put into words. This black and white thinking mirrors our tendency to look at the world in terms of 'all or nothing'. We either find things to be good or bad ... beautiful or ugly ... easy or hard ... happy or sad ... because black and white thinking is the illusion that we have all the answers to life when we really don't. And when we engage in this type of thinking, it can actually cause a lot of unnecessary problems in our life. Magical, mystical or on a mundane level, black and white thinking limits our perspective. When we only see things in black and white, we miss out on alternative ways of viewing the world and these other perspectives may be just as good if not better than our current perspective.

Magical Exercise: Self-pleasuring & sex magic

Do you need a partner of the opposite gender to do sex

magic? Not in most cases. Sex magic relies on blending masculine and feminine energies. When we speak of male and female energies, however, we're not referring to men and women. Everyone, regardless of gender, has *both* masculine and feminine energies: same-sex couples can do sex magic as successfully as opposite-sex couples. And we don't even need a physical partner to perform sex magic. Solo sex (i.e. masturbation) can be very effective - in fact, it may be a good idea to practice alone for a while before we start working with a magical partner.

For many practitioners, the fact that sex magic can be practiced alone is one of its main attractions. *'Although I've experimented with partnered sex magic, I find the solo spells have worked better for me thus far'* says one witch who wishes to remain nameless. One of the biggest misconceptions about sex magic is that the ritual we perform must be directed at some *sexual* result. In reality, we can utilize sex magic to get whatever we want just as we would with any spell-casting. Sexual energy is just energy. So, feel free to visualize … a better job … a book deal … somewhere new to live … as you reach orgasm.

For sex magic we also need to observe the same rules that we would for any Circle working and create a protective/holding area by casting the Compass according to our normal method. The Compass contains the energy we raise until it is time to release it, and stops it from sloshing out of the magic circle and depleting before we're ready to direct it.

Before even thinking of activating a spell, however, there is the *most* important element of the preparation to be taken into consideration – *defining our requirements* and not going off at half-cock. Ambiguity can cause more problems than we need right now, so be focused on *exactly* what it is we are casting for in order to solve our problems.

We think about our *actual* needs and begin by making a list that we will be reviewing, tweaking, altering and amending before it is ready to be incorporated in a real-life sex-magical rite. When we have a clear idea of what we want, we're more likely to get it, and rituals such as sex magic help us do this providing we keep focused on our intent. And remember, the witch has the 'right' to ask but the 'powers that be' have the right to refuse.

To enhance the devotional aspects of our magical masturbation rite, we need to create a seductive setting. We deserve it. Put on some mood music, light candles, or draw a bath, scatter it with rose petals, and masturbate in the tub. Even if we don't really believe in this kind of magic, creating a dreamy night in can be healing in itself. Self-pleasuring, or masturbation is still a taboo subject for many people – men *and* women - and some have no idea of the magical results that are literally a gentle touch away.

Sexual pleasure has countless benefits, yet if we've not done it before, we will probably find ourselves pretty uncomfortable when we attempt it for the first time as a *magical* rite. For many, sexual pleasure, as a whole, has been tainted with shame - and masturbation is still *the* darkest secret. From the time we touch ourselves as curious children, and possibly get slapped on the hand by the adults in our lives, we learn that touching ourselves is wrong. We learn that we shouldn't do it and if we do, we should feel bad about it. Spiritually speaking, sexual feeling and orgasm is one of the best ways to raise our magical potential. There are many who practice sex magic, which creates a powerful intention providing we remain focused on that intention while masturbating. The energy and power created during orgasm infuses the intention with incredible power, thus making the intention more powerful.

Needless to say, in order to perform successful sex magic, we have to remain focused on our goal ... focus on what we want to achieve ... which isn't so easy. Focusing on magical goals and holding them in our mind's eye while the ecstasy mounts is distracting because our body is enjoying the sensation and our brain is screaming ... *this is a magical rite! Concentrate!* At precisely the right moment we release the energy out onto the astral and feel it take flight. We close down the Compass and in having a sweet biscuit and a hot drink we earth ourselves and disperse any psychic residue.

"But," writes magical practitioner, Lisa in the *Elephant Journal:*

...as with anything, with practice you get better. Both at focusing and at speeding up the time to orgasm. (I find it's best to do quick and dirty when doing orgasm magic. Another important thing is I need to make sure I'm not going to be disturbed! Getting a phone call in the middle of masturbating is annoying, sure; getting one in the middle of orgasm magic? You're going to have to start over, probably. In my opinion, orgasm magic is one of the easiest ways to accomplish spell-work. Feel free to experiment, play around, and figure out what works for you.

Or as Woody Allen once said: *'Hey, don't knock masturbation. It's sex with someone I love!'*

Chapter Two

Power of Equilibrium

As British spiritual philosopher, Alan Watts observes in *Nature, Man & Woman:*

> ...*the problem of man's relation to nature raises the problem of man's relation to woman – a matter about which the spiritually-minded members of our own [Western] culture have been significantly 'squeamish' and that 'the Christian world, as we know it, is only a half-world in which the feeling and the symbolic feminine is unassimilated'*

That is, not absorbed or integrated into a wider society or culture.

We also all know that when Christians first distinguished themselves from pagans, the word *pagan* simply meant 'country-dweller' and that the 'greatest challenge was, for as long as fifteen-hundred years, the competition of the tenacious nature religions of the peasantry where every important element in the rural economy took on religious significance'. During the Middle Ages, however, as Professor Jeffrey Richards observes, pre-Christian tribal and peasant society went on its own giddy way and try as they might, there were certain elements in paganism that defied Christian absorption, particularly those immoral fertility cults. In Professor Richards' opinion, overt paganism with strong overtones of magic continued to exist and to be fought by the Church until the ninth century. Medieval homes and communities often lacked privacy, and it might have been difficult for a couple to find a place they could be intimate but medievalist Ruth Mazo Karras suggests that '*the church, safe, dry, and deserted for much of the day, might have been the equivalent of the back seat of a car*'.

The tunnel-visioned authors of the *Malleus Maleficarum* claimed that all witchcraft came from carnal lust *'which is in women insatiable'* and *'all wickedness is but little to the wickedness of a woman'*. In view of this ecclesiastical tendency to focus exclusively on a single, limited objective, it is not surprising that medieval woman clung firmly to her pagan faith which placed male and female at level pegging. St Augustine had been banging on *ad nauseam* about the sins of the flesh and so chastity became *the* Christian virtue; while St Jerome played another blinder with *'A man who is too passionately in love with his wife is an adulterer'*! It wasn't until the late 11th century, however, that the Roman Catholic Church began to impose celibacy upon its clergy. Before this, priests could marry but the notion that they could take a roll in the hay with their wives and then touch the altar and sacrament didn't sit well with higher-ups in the Church.

According to the *Decretum* of Burchard of Worms (c.1025), that we can only describe as a catalogue of error, having intercourse in the missionary position really was the only way to go. Other positions posed the risk of confusing gender roles or emphasizing the pleasurable aspects of the act, rather than its role as the engine of procreation. In fact, those discovered deviating from the standard position faced punishment - depending on the specifics of the transgression that ranged from three year's penance for *'dorsal intercourse with the woman on top'* to ten days on bread and water for male masturbation by hand. *'For the use of a perforated piece of wood, you got twenty days (and probably splinters),'* observed Professor Richards.

These religious prejudices made such strong inroads into pagan belief that even today the bias rears its ugly head as author Nimue Brown points out in 'Sex in Paganism' on her Druid Life Blog.

Sex can be power – if you think about who is allowed to have sex, and who is allowed to enjoy it, the issues of power balance are considerable. For a lot of history, sex has been a part of male power over women, with ignorance and shaming reducing the scope for women to enjoy it. ... Sex is a big concern for religions. Who is allowed to do it, and under what circumstances. If you look at religious laws, what it often comes down to is a way of controlling women's sexual activities so that men can be confident about who the father is. Any religion that encourages people to deny the flesh for the sake of the afterlife tends not to be very keen on sex at all, and will tolerate it only between man and wife for the purposes of producing children. The pleasures of the flesh are often represented as being at odds with spirituality, so in a fair few traditions, dedicating to a spiritual life means celibacy.

The theme here for me, is allowing some people to dictate to other people what their relationship with sex ought to be. Whether it's 'you have to have sex to be initiated' or 'you cannot have the sex you want and be acceptable to god' there are issues of control. We don't have to have sex at Beltaine. As Pagans, we should not feel obliged to do anything sexual, nor obliged not to. Consent is everything. If we're not harming, or abusing someone else, then what we do, or don't do, should be our own business. We can honour the energies of life without having to enact them. We can enact on our own terms should we choose to.

If sex is not celebratory and magical for you, then you need to start from where you are. Feeling pressured to react in a certain way is no kind of liberation, and if Paganism means to hold its head up as a sex-positive spirituality, we must also have room for those who say no.

From an older perspective, Bob Clay-Egerton's no-nonsense approach to occultism is probably the best way of introducing the inevitable subject of sex into the magical equation. '*I may often appear a little harsh towards some of my fellow witches and magicians,*' he wrote. '*It is perhaps that I am getting grouchy in my old age but to be honest one can get a little tired of the rubbish being passed off nowadays as arcane knowledge by posturing poltroons who imagine that to have read a few books on witchcraft and ritual magic makes them 'Masters' of the occult.'*

No doubt the prissy-minded, the undefiled intelligentsia of the pagan world, the plastic pagans, the sham shamans, the wishy-washy witches and the maudlin magicians will wring their hands at the mere suggestion that some aspects of occultism have sexual overtones. From the Craft's point of view it is popularly hailed as an ancient fertility religion ... [although as Robert Cochrane frequently remarked, there had been no cause for a fertility religion in Europe since the advent of the coulter-share plough in the 13th-century.] ... but although fertility is based on sex, some modern witches appear to be ruled by the sexual-moral bias of the religion which persecutes them! It is, they say, a 'sacred act'. It can be, in the right circumstances and with the correct intention. Otherwise it is a very natural act. The primary purpose of all sexual enactment in Tantric and some of the other magical techniques is the raising of power by the manipulation of various wavelengths and energies through the physical and mental stages to affect the spiritual.
[What You Call Time]

The views of religions and religious believers range widely, from giving sex and sexuality a rather negative connotation to believing that sex is the highest expression of the divine. From a purely magical point of view there is nothing wrong with holy or sacred sex. In Wicca and some of the more traditional Paths, the Great Rite is a ritual based on the *hieros gamos*, although it is generally enacted symbolically by a knife blade being placed point first into a chalice, the action symbolizing the union of the male and female divine. *Hieros gamos* or hierogamy is a sexual ritual that plays out a marriage between a god and a goddess, especially when enacted in a symbolic ritual where human participants represent the deities. Before the ritual came in for a lot of media speculation during the 1980s anti-occult campaign, the Great Rite was sometimes carried out in actuality by the High Priest and High Priestess. The notion of *hieros gamos* does not, however, always presuppose literal sexual intercourse in ritual, because is it also used in purely symbolic or mythological context, notably in alchemy and hence in Jungian psychology in *Symbols of Transformation*. But what exactly is sex magic? Skye Alexander, author of *Sex Magic for Beginners* explains:

> *First, let me explain what sex magic isn't. Sex magic isn't some sort of kinky parlor game. It's not intended to jazz up a lackluster love life or increase your chances of getting laid on Saturday night. The main purpose isn't even sexual enjoyment or procreation. Having said all that, however, it's quite likely your intimate relationships and sexual satisfaction will improve as a result of practicing sex magic - that just isn't the primary objective.*
>
> *Sex magic is a means to an end, a way to mobilize the amazing creative power of sexual energy to generate a desired result. Basically, you do sex magic for the same reasons you would do any other type of magic: to cause something you desire to happen. Your goal might be to promote healing, or attract money, or achieve spiritual enlightenment. When you add sexual energy, you increase the intensity of a magic spell. It's like adding more octane to gasoline.*

Sexual instinct and energy are inherent in everyone. Driven by the laws of attraction and repulsion, we are all sexual beings unless damaged by injury (mental, emotional or physical) or illness (when libido may be impaired or removed); or when an individual chooses to be celibate – pouring their sexual energy into other areas under a condition known as sublimation. Pure sex magic is the use of sexual intercourse to raise the spiritual level of the participants. In witchcraft, the couple involved will usually be in a long-standing relationship and this has nothing to do with morality. It is simply because an established couple will know each other so intimately (pun intended) that any shyness, titillation or embarrassment will be put aside and the couple can get on with their serious magical work.

The other form simply uses arousal as a power-raising exercise, and the release of orgasm as a release of that energy to fulfill the magical desires of the witch. In this case, a witch can have sex with a partner who may not even be aware that this is anything more than the normal sex act – because only the active witch needs to keep their mind on the job! Sex magic can also be a solitary experience, but again it is necessary to concentrate on the desired outcome of the ritual and not forget about the point of the exercise at the critical moment. To stay focused throughout a sex magic ritual requires practice and dedication – and great strength of purpose. Arousal and orgasm are simply the *mechanics* by which the magical and spiritual powers are awakened, raised and released.

Some magical workings benefit from a male dominant partner with the female playing a submissive role; while other rites are more successful with the female taking the dominant role and the male remaining submissive, depending on the nature and required outcome of the ritual involved. Nevertheless, unless the dominant partner remains mistress/master of the force they have aroused, they cannot direct it at their objective. In general, in both religious and magical sexual rites the element of pleasure is secondary: it is the means to the end not the end itself. One couple of my acquaintance had thought for years that the whole ritual revolved around them both reaching the finishing post at the same time with multiple orgasms all round. They had a lot of fun trying but never achieved any real magical results in the process. Once there'd been a slight adjustment to the technique of who was dominant/submissive for the purpose of a particular rite they achieved complete magical harmony – and had even more fun practicing!

By this time, the reader will have realized that a great deal of magical practice revolves around what is usually referred to as sexual dynamics – i.e. directing the primordial energies generated *during* a sex act to manifest in both practical and mystical results. This practice, of course, is what gained Aleister Crowley his undeserved reputation in a world that was still recovering from repressive Victorian morality. It should also be emphasized that we are not talking about communal sex and orgiastic behavior: sex magic is more effective with a sympathetic partner, or as a solitary experience.

Using sex as part of a magical discipline requires many years of study and would require a full-length encyclopedia to itself in order to explain the various techniques and subtleties involved in the practice which usually has its roots in the Eastern disciplines of Tantra. The use of sex in magic is merely the means of raising *natural* psychic energy through the act of intercourse – or even as the solitary practice of masturbation. There should be no thought of sexual gratification since the concentration needed to convert the sexual current into magical energy leaves little room for enjoyment or impressive bedroom athletics.

Ritual magic is the harnessing and channeling of polarity, of which sexual energy forms but a small part in terms of human interaction. Although Tantric yoga is now widely written about in the glossy magazines, it is an Eastern system of *spiritual* development that utilises sexual union in a highly disciplined technique. Needless to say, a considerable amount of Crowley's sexual-magical techniques came from the East and his own personal and extensive studies of yoga, but Madame Blavatsky had already witnessed some of these rites and pronounced them mucky. In the 1990s, pop-star Sting made a throw-away comment about seven-hour Tantric sex sessions and nearly thirty years on, the poor soul is still being asked about it by journalists from around the globe!

The application of Tantric yoga as a form of a recreational

or fashion fad should, therefore, be treated as highly suspect because genuine Tantra can be downright dangerous unless the practitioner has been trained to deal with the fire-force released by awakening the *kundalini,* or sleeping snake, at the base of the spine. Its arousal is the goal of an elaborate technique usually taking many years to master. It would therefore be unwise to confuse European sex magic with Tantra, for they do indeed pursue different aims. Tantric practice is always oriented towards worship and mysticism, combing the powers of Shiva and Shakti in order to transcend them; while Western sex magic is oriented more towards the earth element. And it would also be unwise to harbor the belief that sex in ritual is a male preoccupation, as Annie Wyse discovered when running a Tantric workshop many years ago:

> As it happened they were all women and by lunchtime were beginning to ask when the sex would start. They all hoped to be able to masturbate off into some kind of fantasy visualisation (led by me making suggestions), with a 'fantasy god' as a partner. They were very crestfallen when I disillusioned them … I still find it somewhat hard to believe that a dozen women, all ages, would pay a reasonable sum to come along and masturbate with people they'd never met before in their lives … AND believed this was sex magic! Don't you ever go believing it's just men who have their dicks hanging out and wanting their leg over when they first come to a Circle or Tantric workshop. Women can be just the same if not worse; just as randy and just as ignorant. The 'spirit' is not necessarily any more emancipated or enlightened when it inhabits a female body than when it's inside a bloke!

Although female magicians (or sorceresses) have existed since ancient times, women have faced almost insurmountable difficulty in entering the 'fraternity' of the sex magic community. Possibly because there is still a deep-rooted fear or revulsion in the mind of both primitive and modern man for menstrual blood; contact was believed to be highly dangerous and precautionary measures involved their females being isolated or even caged during menstruation. Fortunately, it was also discovered that women generate sexually-magical power during this time. According to *Secrets of the German Sex Magicians* this is precisely how the social taboos concerning menstruation came into being, since this natural occurrence was rarely handled in a controlled manner and patriarchal societies were simply not capable of handling such 'bundles of power'. '*Experience of Western sex magic shows that menstruating women are an immense source of power in a ritual,*' wrote Frater U.D. '*Male sex magicians should rejoice in the opportunity to work with a menstruating female magician, because this can multiply many times the efficacy of sex-magical operations.*'

There is, however, another side to this sex-magic equation as Mishlen Linden explains in her *Typhonian Teratomas: The Shadows of the Abyss* and that is the fact that for the most part the little that has been written on the subject has been written by *men*! Most magical texts claim that a woman's power-time occurs during menstruation – and that is correct from the *male* point of view. During this time the power becomes available to those outside the woman, i.e. her magical partner.

> *In actuality, it is during the days prior to her period in which the power builds. This is the time of empowerment for women. The three days prior to her period can be considered her most powerful, and all the days between the moon-time can be seen as leading up to these three days.*

Linden maintains that the imbalances caused by the suppression of this magical energy results in PMT – pre-menstrual tension – as the body builds up excess energy like an old-fashioned pressure cooker. '*... the body, buffeted by its increased power, tries desperately to equalise the force building within. This gradually results in more* *imbalances which are the root causes of PMT.'*

Good old *Man, Myth & Magic* upheld the magical view of sex as a way of apprehending and achieving unity, not only in human beings but in the world at large. This belief is, of course, not confined to practicing magicians. An increasing number of people consider sexual activity to be good, not just because it is pleasurable, but because it will somehow, magically and mystically promote general peace and harmony. This merely brings up-to-date the old principle that by imitative magic, human sexual acts promote the beneficent activities of the gods.

In general, when practicing with a partner, communication is very important. Because we should either work together completely or keep our partner entirely in the dark about the fact that we're manifesting magic during intercourse. *'Either they know what it is that you're doing, or they shouldn't know at all. Because any person who kind of knows and isn't really into it can fuck up the whole flow of energy,'* Bri Luna of the Hoodwitch Blog explains. *'So either keep them ignorant altogether, or they know and they are going to focus on that energy as well, so it makes it that much more powerful if you are going to come together.'*

Magical Exercise

Obviously, there's more to sex magic than making mad, passionate love day and night. Sex magic is both an art and a skill and like any art or skill, it requires learning certain techniques, then practicing those techniques to build magical ability.

The first step is to slow down – mentally as well as physically. Most of us tend to rush toward orgasm, rather than pacing ourselves during sex but drawing out the experience and allowing our sexual energy to build gradually enhances our magical power. In *Sex Magic for Beginners*, Skye Alexander has this suggestion for a couple adopting a joint responsibility for raising the necessary power to be directed towards a magical goal:

Let your excitement slowly increase until you feel almost ready to come. Then back off. Do some deep breathing. Shift from genital stimulation to stroking other parts of the body: arms, back, feet, and so on. When the immediacy has subsided, gradually elevate the level of excitation until, once again, you almost reach the point of no return. Ease off again. Continue in the manner for as long as you like, slowly and steadily building intensity. With practice, you'll learn to 'stay on the edge' for an extended period of time.

During this period of high arousal, keep your telos [goal] in mind. The more intense your feelings, the faster you can attract what you desire, and in this near-orgasmic state your magnetic power is tremendous. You don't have to focus keenly on your objective all the time, but remain aware of your purpose for engaging in this sexual ritual. As you raise energy and cycle it through your body, mentally attach your intention to that energy.

When you're finally ready to release the energy you've built up, hold your telos clearly in your mind and feel the pleasure of having your desired outcome manifested in your life. Then let your orgasm wash through you. As it does, it sweeps your intention before it, like a wave pushing a boat along on its crest. The momentum you've generated carries your telos out into the universe ... After orgasm, relax and stop thinking about your telos. Enjoy the calm after the tempest. Allow the universe to do its part now.

As we've discussed earlier in the chapter, however, some magical workings benefit from a male dominant partner with the female playing a submissive role; while other rites are more successful with the female taking the dominant role and the male remaining submissive, depending on the nature and required outcome of the ritual involved. Nevertheless, unless the dominant partner remains mistress/master of the force they have aroused, they cannot direct it at their objective at the right moment ... and has nothing to do with any gender superiority.

Chapter Three

Every Man and Every Woman is a Star

The common misperceptions around all forms of sexuality continue to exist in many people and places, and very few have even considered the possibility that sexuality can be used to enhance spiritual growth. That in matters of sacred sexuality, the energy or essence of the people involved is more important than the physical bodies they inhabit. *'The division of life onto the high and lower categories of spirit and nature usually goes hand in hand with a symbolism in which the spirit is male and nature female,'* wrote Alan Watts in *Nature, Man & Woman*.

> *The importance of the correspondence between spirit and man and nature and woman is that it projects upon the world as a disposition in which the members of several cultures, including our own, are still involved. It is a disposition in which the split between man and nature is related to a problematic attitude to sex, though like egg and hen it is doubtful which came first. It is perhaps best to treat them as arising mutually, each being symptomatic of the other.'*
>
> *The historical reasons for our problematic attitude to sexuality are so obscure that there are numerous contradictory theories to explain it ... The fact is that in some unknown way the female sex has become associated with the earthy aspect of human nature and with sexuality as such. The male sex could conceivably have been put in the same position, and there is no conclusive evidence that women are more desirous and provocative of sexual activity than men, or vice versa. These are almost certainly matters of cultural conditioning which do not explain how the culture itself came to be as it is.*

This is especially true when we look at certain aspects of

human history throughout the ancient world. For example, generally speaking, Anglo-Saxon England was a golden age of independence, power, wealth, and education for women. Below the ruling class, the woman had a right to refuse her suitor and even if she agreed, her family would ensure that a marriage agreement was drawn up to her advantage. There was a bride price, but this was not given to the bride's family but to the woman herself on the morning after the wedding, to do with as she wished.

Laws also made clear that within a marriage the finances were held to be the property of both husband and wife and not of the husband alone. Earlier laws even ensured that a woman could walk out of a marriage which did not please her and if she took the children with her, she was entitled to take half the property - a right not re-established until the 20th century. But most of this came to an end with the Norman Conquest and its introduction of the continental version of Christianity, where women were considered inferior to men.

Going further back in time, Spartan women were afforded a public education as well, but this was very radical since other Greek girls were not formally educated. They could not, however, use their education to have careers or earn money. Their income likely came from land holdings that either they or their families were given through a public land distribution program. Land ownership for women in the Greek world was certainly unheard of. Another freedom that Spartan women had over other Greek women was their ability to fraternize in public with Spartan men. Along with exercising with the opposite sex came the ability to trade conversation and political witticisms with them.

In fact, Spartan women were notoriously known for their razor-sharp wit and outspoken natures. This freedom turned heads amongst the other Greeks *poleis*, and they, of course, disapproved greatly. But if the physical health of a Spartan woman was seen as vital to her ability to produce strong Spartan boys, then her mental and intellectual might have been seen as just as important. Bearing and raising children was considered the most important role for women in Spartan society but it placed them on an *equal* footing with male warriors in the Spartan army. When Sparta deteriorated in the 4th century BC, their fall from grace was blamed in part on the inclusion of their women in public life, their ability to own land, and thus their supposed ability to exert a certain amount of power over their men.

Still in the ancient world, women in ancient Egypt had some special rights other women did not have in other comparable societies. They could own property and were, at court, legally equal to men. However, ancient Egypt was a society dominated by men: women could not have important positions in administration and were also excluded from ruling the country, though there are some significant exceptions! Nevertheless, Egyptian women could have their own businesses, own and sell property, and serve as witnesses in court cases. Unlike most women in the Middle East, they were even permitted to socialize with men. They could escape bad marriages by divorcing and remarrying. And were entitled to one third of the property their husbands owned. The political and economic rights Egyptian women enjoyed made them the most liberated females of their time.

One of our Coven members has native American ancestry and she brought this humorous story to the discussion ... The Red Road of the Lakota *oyate* which is essentially a prehistoric way of life, is male oriented, we have Unci Maka mother earth, but above her is father sky whom we call Wakan Tanka - the Great Spirit. He is first in all things, he is light, thunder, life and death, joy, mourning, wildness, freedom and so much more; but Unci Maka is the deep mystery of birth and death, the darkness, pain, suffering and ecstatic from which we come, and to whom we will return. They complement each other and tumble through the stars locked in an eternal embrace. Without one, the other cannot exist, and one of them has to be the front-man, and as an old Lakota proverb tells it: '*When the world was new, Hapi asked the first people if they would be alright. 'Oh yes,' said the man, 'for I will always have the first say'*. The woman smiled and said '*But I will always have the last say.*' In this way we see that although it may seem that the Lakota are a patriarchal society, we are in fact more matriarchal for although the men lead, it is the women, the life givers who steer us on our path for they are the teachers and that is why they always have the last say.

> *When therefore we shall speak loosely of the reasons for certain attitudes, we shall not be speaking of fundamental historical causes ... We shall be speaking of the reasons as they exist today, either of matters of open knowledge or as forms of unconscious conditioning. There is no clear evidence that we are unconsciously conditioned by events from the remote historical past ... Certainly we can trace the historical effects of Christian, Buddhist, or Hindu doctrines upon our sexual attitudes, but what lies behind these doctrines and the attitudes from which they arose remains conjectural and dim. Furthermore, it is always possible to argue not that we are conditioned by the past, but that we use the past to condition ourselves in the present and for reasons which are not historical but deeply inward and unknown...* [Nature, Man & Woman]

So, although we can trace Christian misogyny to grubby little monks with their ink stained fingers, misandry (the hatred of, contempt for, or prejudice against men in general) is a much more recent innovation. Misandry may be manifested in numerous ways, including social exclusion, sex discrimination, hostility, gynocentrism, matriarchy, belittling of men, violence against men, and sexual objectification. Such attitudes may be normalised culturally, such as through humour at the expense of men, or blaming all world problems on 'men', or suggesting that men are redundant.

Religious studies professors Paul Nathanson and Katherine Young examined the institutionalization of misandry in the public sphere in their 2001 three-book series *Beyond the Fall of Man*, which refers to misandry as a 'form of prejudice and discrimination that has become institutionalized in North American society', writing: *'The same problem that long prevented mutual respect between Jews and Christians - the teaching of contempt - now prevents mutual respect between men and women'.*

In *Psychology Today*, Joe Kort, a certified sex therapist writes that words can and do wound since they perpetuate norms that give rise to bigotry, misogyny, misandry, racism, homophobia, and more.

I've even heard women say things like, 'Balls are gross. I hate them'. If a woman overheard men talking about vaginas being dirty and disgusting, she'd surely think this was misogyny and microaggression, but why not the other way around? Many otherwise enlightened people seem to think that putting a man down by shaming him for the transgressions of a few criminal types, or for his inadequate physicality, is a sort of privilege or entitlement. They are not even aware of their misandry.

Mostly we know that men, especially heterosexual white men, have a privileged status in our society, that they are mostly blind to their privilege, and that we live in a patriarchal world. We often think of patriarchy as hurting women, but we don't talk about how it also hurts men. Patriarchy includes a rigid standard of looks and behaviour, and men who fail to follow the standard are tormented ruthlessly. Conforming men may be 'blind to their privilege', but nerds and sissies are fair targets for contempt.

Even the absence of online discussions of microaggressions against men is itself a microaggression because the absence renders the problem invisible. Some discussions of microaggressions toward women and minorities even say that because men are privileged they can't experience microaggressions. But many men are not privileged. These men have been rendered invisible and at the same time marked as fair game. [Psychology Today]

Any form of sexual bias has always been frowned upon within traditional British Old Craft because it reveals a complete lack of magical awareness and/or proficiency on the part of the newcomer. Witchcraft has, over the years, had its fair share of predatory males *and* females but the problem was usually rooted out by the Elders of the various Traditions, and the offenders exposed, so to speak. Especially when it came down to 'you can't be initiated without having sex', or 'that's how the magic is passed down from male to female, and vice versa' brigade who usually weren't even initiates themselves!

One young woman was rabidly misandrous despite the fact that we make no secret of the fact that Old Craft is unapologetic about being god-oriented and Magister-led in its practices. We were assured that she had no problem with this but only weeks into her training we found that it wasn't possible to hold a conversation or conduct a lesson without her vagina creeping into the equation! She pulled no punches in proclaiming loudly and at every opportunity that she hated half the world's population, rich and poor, kind and cruel, black and white, gay and straight, just because they happen to have the Y-chromosome! It goes without saying that she was asked to leave since her social views and values were at odds with our Old Craft belief in the equality of the sexes.

Another common problem are the middle-aged women who, within weeks of beginning their studies, are continuously harping on about the sexual shenanigans they've heard are associated with Craft Initiation. Will they have to appear naked in front of everyone? Will the Magister perform the rite of Initiation? Will they be required to participate in group sex? Like most ordinary Crafters, I am aware that such non-typical human nature existed and while some sex differences are biological, men and women are psychologically similar – far more similar than they are different.

Aleister Crowley, is the most famous 19th century occultist who viewed sex as 'the supreme magical power'. Contemporary witches more often than not, dismiss much of his work but any serious student of magic (or *magick*) male or female, can learn much from his writing. In the commentary for *The Law Is For All*, there is an extremely interesting eulogy for the woman who follows the Thelemic path, which Crowley's critics choose to ignore when they accuse him of chauvinism:

We of Thelema say the 'Every man and every woman is a Star.' We do not fool and flatter women; we do not despise and abuse them. To us a woman is Herself, absolute, original, independent, free, self-justified, exactly as a man is.

We dare not thwart Her Going, Goddess she! We arrogate no right upon Her will; we claim not to deflect Her destiny. She is Her own sole arbiter; we ask no more than to supply our strength to Her ...'

We do not want Her as a slave; we want Her free and royal, whether Her love fight death in our arms by night, or Her loyalty ride by day beside us in the Charge of the Battle of Life.

So sayeth this our Book of the Law. *We respect woman in the self of Her own nature; we do no arrogate the right to criticize Her. We welcome Her as our ally; come to our camp as Her Will, free-flashing, sword-swinging, hath told Her, Welcome, thou Woman, we hail thee, star shouting to Star!*

Crowley's Scarlet Woman was, of course, the Goddess herself on a higher plane and on a more earthy level, a medium directly in touch with the gods. In her lower state, she was Babalon, the spiritual consort of the Beast 666 on which she rode [*The Book of Thoth*]. In her higher state she was Shakti *'with whom she was locked in an eternal embrace of continuous orgasm. From which came the foundation of the Universe'.*

Whether we like to admit it or not, sex is a natural element of witchcraft and since time immemorial, witches have been harnessing their sexual energy to do magic. Given the preponderance of love spells and evil-yet-seductive witches in pop-art culture, it's understandable that sex magic is so often misunderstood. Sarane Alexandrian was a French philosopher, essayist, and art critic, a member of the surrealist group in Paris in the years directly after World War II and author of more than sixty books, including several on occultism and art. In the chapter 'The Higher Science of Sacred Sexuality' he wrote:

A path has been laid that allows the spiritual teachers of our time to incorporate sex magic into their teaching and to instruct their disciples on how to use sex to go beyond pleasure and toward individual omnipotence ... The schools of Gnosis, the Kabbalah, the Cathars, the Templars, the Freemasons, and the Rosicrusians were 'initiatory organisations', and it was inspired by these models that the adepts of magical eroticism blended rituals into their sexual practice, in order for it to be a mystic quest of the sacred nature of the flesh – not simple libertinism. [The Great Work of the Flesh]

Magical Exercise

There are two human elements that can be harnessed to add impetus to magic working: anger and sex. Most modern Craft treatise will pontificate at length about the dubious outcome connected to magical workings fuelled by anger but is this always correct? We're not talking about a petty, spiteful reaction but that talked about in 'A Case for Anger and Magic' by The Witches Next Door ...

Anger. Seething, frothing, steam coming out of the ears like an old time cartoon character whose head turns into a boiling kettle,

44

kind of Anger. Ever felt that? Feeling it now? My guess is that somewhere along the line, you've been told by a parent, a teacher, a mentor or a spiritual adviser that anger won't really serve you or your community. Yes, much of the time, that's probably great advice, but not always. There's a case for anger. And perhaps, anger can teach us something about our witchcraft that is ever so important.

Some Pagan thinking (maybe borrowing from the New Age movement), often frames 'negative' emotions as if they should be banished and sent away without notice. There's a tendency to sweep problematic emotions under the rug and smile and sit in the warmth of the sunshine. When did witchcraft begin including this fantasy that an evolution of the spirit means we walk perpetually in the light, espousing a never ending stream of positive affirmations, in a constant state of magical bliss? Well, sorry to tell you, but witchcraft was not born out of the need to make nice with the new neighbours. Witchcraft was and is the practice of making things happen. [Patheos Blog]

Getting magically stoked up by anger, especially at the dark of the moon, and we *can* move mountains. But as a couple in our Coven recently discovered, in the short time it took to construct the rite, the anger had dissipated. Around the same time, another member was talking about 'carefully controlled anger' used in magic – which is a contradiction in terms if ever I heard one! Anger, beautiful, white-hot, bubbling volcanic anger needs to be utilized while it is in 'raving, ripping, rending mode' if it is going to be at all effective. However …

… it isn't possible to simulate molten fury but in magical practice orgasms are considered to be the ultimate magical force. We can attempt to throw any spell we want using sex magic, but, the first thing to remember is that it's important to set a clear intention while meditating on the desired outcome, enabling us

to understand what we truly want. When you begin, Kristen Sollee, author of Witches, Sluts, Feminists: Conjuring the Self Positive suggests tuning 'into the goal you have in mind and channel all of the electric energy of your orgasm into that visualization. This will allow your energy to mystically connect with your intention and give it power, potentially enabling it to come true.

If working as a couple, it is the dominant partner's responsibility for raising the power during intercourse and directing it towards the intended goal at the moment of his/her partner's orgasm. The dominant partner should be the 'injured party' rather than the one who's taken umbrage on their partner's behalf. If nothing else, this exercise demonstrates why magic works best when an established couple are involved and the passive partner knows that his/her turn will come when the roles are reversed to enhance another magical working in the future.

Modern adherents of sex magic have a myriad of historical, cultural practices to draw inspiration from, and many of them emphasize the importance of finding what works best for us individually. In many ways, sex magic is similar to any other form of energy work, which harnesses energy, with the practitioner often tapping into our own spiritual energy (or god-power): the only difference is that the energy being harnessed in this case is released to coincide with orgasm.

Chapter Four

The 'W' Word

As Alan Watts observes in *Nature, Man & Woman*:

> *Let us say that in the Christian and post-Christian West we simply find ourselves in a culture where nature is called Mother Nature, whereas God is exclusively male, and where one of the common meanings of Woman or Women with a capital 'W' is simply sex, whereas Man with the capital 'M' means humanity in general.*

We should also briefly look at what Sarene Alexandrian refers to as *'the love-spell tradition'* which appears on everyone's witch-list because the most common magic in antiquity and the Middle Ages was the sort used to help unhappy lovers. Its principal purpose was to manufacture beverages, powders and mixtures that a man or woman would administer to the individual who they could not otherwise induce to fall in love with them. And it would appear that these are still as popular today since a quick Google search on the internet comes up with an impressive 107,000,000 results! One delightful recipe from an 18th-century manuscript, *Secrets pour se faire aimer* recommends:

> *Take three hairs from your balls and three from your left armpit and burn them on a very hot stove shovel, and once they are burned, put them into a piece of bread that you will place in soup or coffee … The young girl or woman to whom you have given this will be convinced that she will never leave you.*

The original date-rape drug can also be found in a recipe calling for female mandrake, that *'in autumn has violet flowers, bluish green flowers, and reddish sap-filled fruits'*. It was medicinal herb used by apothecaries. A nuptial wine was made from it and offered on her wedding day to a young girl married against her will; after she drank it, she would not feel any revulsion at allowing her spouse to deflower her. Apart from being highly poisonous, the *mandragora* has potent sedative and pain-killing properties and in 1877 it became an official homeopathic preparation in early surgery. Culpeper merely refers to it as a dangerous plant.

Alexandrian also tells us that, although not commonly known, the seer Nostradamus provided a recipe for an *'amorous potion'* that he claimed was a philter invented by Medea and subsequently in common usage throughout Thessaly. The potion was administered by the exchange of saliva during a kiss, and he goes on to say that if some of this potion is swallowed by accident without going into the mouth of the lusted-after individual, it was essential to make love with someone else that same day otherwise the increase of semen it creates will rise into the brain and drive him mad. Alexandrian comments that a glass of champagne would probably be more convenient than this concoction containing magnet powder and jellied octopus suckers preserved in honey!

And as Professor Kieckhefer informs us in *Magic in the Middle Ages*, when medieval writers wanted to cite a classical example of magic, one of the tales they were most likely to recall was from Homer's *Odyssey*, where Odysseus land on the island of the seductive sorceress Circe, who was a dab hand at preparing magical potions:

The literature of Greek and Roman antiquity was often conceived as contributions to Western culture, and these writings are important because they develop the stereotypes of the female magician or witch. In this early literature, as centuries later in trials for witchcraft, the witch tends to be either a young seductress using her magic to promote her amorous purposes or else an ugly hag with awesome and sinister power. Neither of these persistent stereotypes is designed to flatter women, even if the seduction motif could be more sympathetic in tone.

While there is no reason to think that women alone practiced magic, both pagan and Christian writers ascribed it primarily to them, and as a result, this relegation of sexuality and nature to the forces of evil grows out of ignoring the background and fastening upon the stereotype. By associating sex with evil the *'great delight is made an even greater fascination for the other members of a prurient society and sowing the seeds for all the refinements of civilized lust'* according to Dr Watts.

Moralists often saw women especially as prone to magic and superstition because of their supposed moral and intellectual weakness. In fact, the general culture portrayed women as having weak intellect and will, and although earlier literature seldom singled women out as specifically inclined toward witchcraft, the misogynist witchcraft treatise the *Malleus Maleficarum* routinely did so. Image the mortification of those inky-fingered medieval clerics if they learned of the true spiritual and mystical prowess of those morally and intellectually enfeebled witch-women!

For starters, witches have from the earliest times rejected the uncompromising monotheistic god in favour of a more pantheist approach to deity that does not recognize a distinct personal god, anthropomorphic or otherwise. For the pantheist, god is the non-personal divinity that pervades all existence. It is the divine Unity of the world. Coven of the Scales has always been god/male oriented, which often causes problems with newcomers who believe that the goddess is 'All'. Call us old-fashioned but we still believe in the gender dynamics that have powered witchcraft since time immemorial – and which does not lend itself to gender politics because the differences and similarities between the sexes are all part of understanding the equilibrium of magical working. But *both* the Dame and the Magister must be fully capable of running the show ... and this means raising, channeling and directing the power raised within the Compass – whether it be god/male or goddess/female energy.

In a perfectly run coven, the Magister's job is to support the Dame – who is often his wife and who has usually trained as his magical partner – and to represent the god within the Compass. Once again, this has nothing to do with morality but because this established magical partnership is compatible on many different levels, especially if the pair have trained and undergone Initiation at the same time, which makes them truly elect. Problems can arise if Dame and Magister *aren't* magically congruent – where one is less magically competent or experienced than the other: i.e. following a divorce, for example. The most common difficulty arises when a new partner is introduced to the coven and expects to be automatically accepted in the senior role without having a proven track-record.

During the autumn and winter months the Magister is also the symbolic guardian of the goddess as she sleeps and whereas during the spring and summer the Coven rituals are usually Dame-led, during autumn and winter it's the Magister's duty to lead the rites, which are by token more masculine in essence through the turning of the year until Candlemas. Perhaps it is understandable why it is difficult for many pagans/Wiccans to get to grips with Old Craft practice that refuses to be emasculated – even for form's sake! Similarly, this approach also goes a long way to explain why some magical workings benefit from a male-dominant partner with the female playing a submissive role; while other seasonal rites are more successful with the female taking the dominant role and the male remaining submissive, depending on the nature of the magic/power involved and the purpose of the spell-casting. [*Round About the Cauldron Go*]

In truth, Old Craft views its gods in the abstract – the Old Lass and the Old Lad - placing its faith in the Ancestors, who are an amalgam of our culture, traditions, heritage, lineage and antecedents. In general, they are seen as Craft Elders, treated and referred to in much the same way as the most senior of living Elders of a coven or magical group but with additional mystical and magical powers. Sometimes they are identified with the Holy Guardian Angel, the Mighty Dead, the Watchers, or the Old Ones, who gave magical knowledge to mankind, rather than merely family or tribal dead. Or, even more ambiguously 'those who have gone before' - their magical essence distilled into the universal subconscious of witchcraft at differing levels. Reverence for Craft Ancestors is part of the ethic of respect for those who have preceded us in life, and their continued presence on the periphery of our consciousness means that they are always with us. And because traditional witchcraft is essentially a practical thing, the Ancestors are also called upon to help find solutions to magical problems through divination, path-working and spell-casting.

The allocation of an anthropomorphic identity is an ancient teaching tool, whereby many of the gods were originally abstract concepts rather than actual 'god pictures' and, in ancient Egypt in particular many of the later deities were theological images represented by a distinct hieroglyph. As the need for visual images grew, so did the need for more tangible forms on which to focus the people's devotions. The common man's mind dwelt on the concrete, not the abstract and so the gods took on the various cultural humanoid-animal shapes to satisfy the religious teaching-by-pictures demands of less scholarly folk. The ancient image of Pan, with his lusty appetite and goat's horns didn't need much tinkering to transform him into the Christian Devil!

Along the way, in the evolution of contemporary man a raw instinctual value has been lost ... 'and at a deep level the root cause is a disconnection between man and Mother Earth!' opines *Psychology Pathways*. '*It would appear that in the evolution of man from the primitive 'hunter-gatherer' to the more conventional role within a family of being a 'provider', a raw instinctual advantage has been lost in man.*' The 'Marlboro Man' advertising controversy mirrored these sentiments in that the rugged landscape '*was conceived by the middle classes in America as evoking the universal constancy of geological and mythic America beyond politics and ideology, appealing to 'timeless values' ... Landscape images are the last preserve of a nation's myths about nature, civilisation and beauty'*.

Darrell Winfield, who personified the cigarette brand for twenty years, was the ideal poster-child for the rugged, independent self-image of the Wild West. Though there were dozens of Marlboro men over the years, the campaign recruits preceding Winfield were typically screen actors and professional models. Winfield was the real deal. He continued working on ranches well into his modeling career, eventually using his income to move his family onto their own ranch in Wyoming. He epitomised the macho image of resilience, self-sufficiency, independence and free enterprise and unlike some of the other Marlboro men, Winfield had been a cowboy his entire life. In a rare interview he once commented: '*The image they try to portray is more that of ... a kind of rugged individual. It makes us a little more mysterious, but maybe that's not the right word. It's as close to authentic as they can make it.*'

It was probably that very mysterious, macho image rather than the growing anti-smoking lobby, that ignited the wrangle (if you'll excuse the pun) because it portrayed a man at ease with himself in that very wilderness he had supposedly alienated himself from. And the 1980s urban feminist couldn't allow that kind of mystery to go unchallenged. In rural communities, girls and boys are natural competitors in the hunting, shooting, fishing stakes with the girls often out-riding and out-shooting the boys. And it is probably this urban/rural divide that is the real cause of the division between the sexes rather than any gender or age gap.

The traditional elements of witchcraft are generally looked upon as rural pursuits and more openly practiced in the countryside where the parish-pump witch, wise-woman and cunning man culture thrived right into the 20th-century. Since the millennium, however, there has been an overwhelming intellectual stagnation that has become the vanguard of modern paganism and this *is* now reflected in a great deal of Craft instruction of the present day. So many people, who should be on the same side, squabble over details of which path is superior without recognizing that every tradition teaches differently. And that change *is* inevitable if we want Craft to continue to survive.

And growth *is* important to pagan thought. It's okay to be using a certain stepping stones of ideology for a while but if we remain in the same mind-set at 80-years of age, or 60, or 40 as we were at 20, what have we actually learned along the way? How much have we grown spiritually? And how much of an impact can we make when we dismiss something because we have proclaimed to understand it fully while never recognising the difficulties and importance of its impact on our current Craft lifestyle? For example:

Millennials (those born between 1980-1996) who, in their own words, are 'zero tolerant' and have been drawing a much harsher line for anything they consider even slightly inappropriate, will not be comfortable with the tenets of Old Craft and its god/male orientation. Very few of this age-group apply to Coven of the Scales for training, simply because their uncompromising attitude is not even interested in finding out what makes a *genuine* traditional British Old Craft coven tick. They want to tear up the 'rule book' and reinvent what they think witchcraft is all about; resenting the fact that Old Crafters are just as uncompromising when it comes to our beliefs and practices with its 'how can you teach yourself what you don't know exists?' attitude.

Generation X (those born between 1965 and 1979) who came to maturity before the new politics arrived with such gusto, make up the bulk of our students and members having spent many years in neo-pagan/Wiccan groups. Social research describes Gen Xers as: independent, resourceful, self-managing, adaptable, cynical, pragmatic, skeptical of authority, and as seeking a work-life balance. Typically perceived to be disaffected and directionless due to the pursuit of some ill-defined New Age spirituality in their hey-day, the Gen Xers take to the clearly-defined tenets of Old Craft like middle-aged ducks to water.

Baby Boomers (those born between 1946 and 1964) form the Old Guard of traditional witchcraft and consider themselves the guardians of this sacred knowledge. All this might sound as if the writer is sneering or criticising, but this is not the case. If anything, this is a lament for the heady alterno-culture of our own witchlet days when it was necessary to go out and search for *everything*. In seedy back-street occult shops, second-hand bookstores and alternative-press magazines … it was hard work, but it *was* possible and it *was* fun – whilst being a tremendous challenge! One step eventually led to another until the hallowed portals of Atlantis Bookshop, The Sorcerer's Apprentice and Watkins Books led on to higher things … Nowadays it is increasingly difficult even for genuinely interested seekers to find anything that hasn't been oversimplified, diluted, or made frivolous to the degree that modern witchcraft is a pale imitation of what it once was – even in our day!

One Coven of the Scales Elder recently made the remarkable observation that with her continuous Old Craft background she used to look down on those who hadn't been schooled in that discipline; later she felt sorry for them because they hadn't had the same advantages as herself, in being able to access traditional Old Craft teaching early in her studies. She tried being more charitable while subtly offering guidance, but this was usually met with resentment and accusations of elitism, not to mention dismissal as being outdated. Her eventual conclusion was that a large number of contemporary card-carrying pagans prefer the easy way out and it really wasn't worth taking the trouble trying to enlighten them.

Nevertheless, we can't get very far in reading about modern witchcraft without being told that it derives from an ancient fertility religion ... *Oh yeah!?* Because to repeat Robert Cochrane's famous observation that there had been no cause for a fertility religion in Europe since the advent of the coultershare plough in the 13th-century, and that little has been done to correct this impression amongst the pagan community who continue to trot out the trite platitude for the media. Cochrane was highly critical of the development of modern Craft and in an article written as early as 1964 for *Pentagram* ('The Craft Today'), he said he felt that *'many witches had turned their backs on the reality of the outside world, pursuing a belief system that failed to recognize the needs of modern living, while repeating rituals by rote, rather than by understanding'*. In consequence he believed that much of it had become *'static and remote from its original purpose, which was to enlighten the follower spiritually'*. In a further article for *Pentagram* ('The Faith of the Wise') he attacked the limited perception of the various 'authorities' on witchcraft:

> *It is one of the oldest of religions, and also one of the most potent, bringing as it does, Man into contact with Gods, and Man into contact with Self. As such, the Faith is a way of life different and distinct from any theory promulgated by the authorities or historians ... It has, in common with all great religions, an inner experience that is greater than the exterior world. It is a discipline that creates from the world an enriched inward vision. It can and does embrace the totality of human experience from birth to death, then beyond. It creates within the human spirit a light that*

brightens all darkness, and which can never again be extinguished. It is never fully forgotten and never fully remembered.

Witchcraft, however, has always been associated with **sex** in the public mind. And as if to endorse this, a quick Google search came up with 18,800,000 results for 'sex and witchcraft' but if that's not enough to make our heads spin, try actually reading the garbage posted in the comments! All the old, well-worn clichés come trotting out in a typical Craft 'dog and pony show' and it really makes us wonder where these people who claim to be real witches, received their training.

Despite the blatantly obvious excess of love spells that are geared towards finding new men and getting rid of old ones, not to mention spells to attract them in the first place and arouse passion, very few contain warnings about being careful what the seeker asks for! In this category, that Google search coming up with those 107,000,000 results are guaranteed to give any self-respecting witch conniptions. After all, what is a love spell but an indiscriminate astral call for a bit of extra nooky ... but it's got absolutely nothing to do with the spiritual side of traditional witchcraft.

Witchcraft is the harnessing of natural energies for the purpose of directing the Will into creating changes for the better. And in terms of magic, the solitary practitioner is a bit of a fallacy since all magic requires equilibrium - a state in which opposing forces or influences are balanced before the catalyst brings about a result. Since we are discussing the sexual dynamics within magic what better example to give than that weapon of love/lust - the bow and arrow.

In classical mythology, the best-known archers are Eros and Cupid, the Greek and Roman gods of love, respectively. They wield a bow with arrows that cause uncontrollable desire in whomever they hit. It's a beautiful metaphor and what has made Cupid probably the most-depicted archer in art history. There is, of course, a darker side to these myths. Apollo was always 'the Golden Boy', portrayed as a virile youth with flowing golden hair. His bow and love of music played on his lyre were special to him, but Apollo did have a nastier side because Apollo and his sister were capable of acting with cruelty and vindictiveness. Artemis fell in love with a hunter named Orion. Apollo challenged her to an archery match to shoot at what looked like a mere speck in the distance. Artemis was very competitive, so rose to the bait, aiming straight at the target, only to find out too late that she had killed Orion. Neither was Apollo lucky in love. His first love was Daphne, and Eros caused problems with that relationship. Apollo mocked Eros's archery abilities, so Eros shot a golden love arrow into Apollo's heart, and an anti-love one into Daphne's …

Symbolically, the bow and arrow, if not overt phallic emblems, are at least so closely connected with the idea of maleness, together with vigour and authority. Mythological imagery abounds of the bow as the symbol of power and strength. This is not unusual, because in ancient times, the bow and arrow was one of the main weapons of battle, and those with the most skill in using this weapon were often the most feared and powerful. Arrows also signified direction, force, movement, power and direction of travel. When an arrow pointed to the left it meant warding off evil, pointing to the right meant protection and an arrow pointing down meant peace. A pair of crossed arrows on the Coven Stang signified that the Coven was under the dominion of the Old Lad.

The archer is the catalyst between bow and arrow, together with the knowledge and craftsmanship that is required to fire the weapon correctly, and the understanding of the importance of matching the arrows to the bow. Mismatched arrows may not fly correctly or accurately. A more magical analogy is never dry fire a bow. Dry firing means that we shoot without an arrow in place. This can cause lots of damage to the bow, because when we pull back the string energy is stored with the bow, and without the mass of the arrow to absorb the elastic energy released, that energy is instead dissipated through vibration of the bowstring and the bow limbs, and can do significant structural damage to the bow itself. If we cast a magic spell without the proper preparation and directive (or half-hearted measures) then we can fall short of our target, or fail to fire the missile at all.

In terms of magical application, it is also important to attain the proper balance point on an arrow that has been fletched with the point attached. Fletching is the fin-shaped aerodynamic stabilization device attached on arrows, crossbow bolts, or darts. It's typically made from light, semi-flexible materials such as feathers, and each piece of the fin is a 'fletch', also known as a flight or feather. This balance point is very precise, and located about 10-16% of the distance forward from the center of the arrow toward the point. If our arrow (magic) is too lightweight, it may cause the archer to essentially dry fire the bow. As with the bow and arrow, we become the willing catalyst in the form of the skilled and powerful hands of the great archer.

Similarly, masculine and feminine energy has *nothing* to do with gender, and both male and female can tap into essences that Jung referred to as the *anima* – the female element in the male unconscious and *animus* as the male element in the female unconscious. This inner duality is often symbolised by a hermaphrodite figure, like the crowned hermaphrodite depicted in 17th-century alchemical manuscripts, or various portrayals of 'the Lovers' in the Tarot.

Typically, one of these energies is dominant; hence a man and woman can be predominantly feminine *or* masculine. We *all* have masculine and feminine energy in our bodies. Feminine energy is flowing and dynamic: it can't be predicted or always explained with the rational mind. It is unrestricted by the social norms because it doesn't follow any rules other than guidance coming from the heart because the feminine energy doesn't need to get out into the world to get what it wants. It comes her way, which is why the female element of witchcraft has always been judged to be extremely powerful and so feared by the clerics who wrote their anti-witch manuals. Those medieval Churchmen didn't *understand it* but they sure as hell instinctively *felt it* and that was why 'it' (or its practitioners) was consigned to the flames!!

By contrast masculine energy is stable and more predictable. Its strengths are willpower, clarity, and focus. The masculine energy likes to create structures and rules, so it knows how to apply the logic correctly. Another way to look at the masculine energy is as knowledge whereas the feminine is *knowing*. The knowledge is static with precise dimensions and exact design; while *knowing* is forever changing. It's not a *level* of knowledge to be achieved because once you get there, it opens new possibilities and thus inspires you to grow further, especially within the various witchcraft Traditions. Masculine energy is protective; thus, it can sense danger from afar and make sure that nothing threatens him or his loved ones. He fights for what he loves. This is the embodiment of the Horned God watching over the Primal Goddess as she sleeps.

Or, as life-coach Jim Self in his article on 'The Truth About Masculine and Feminine Energy' explains:

> I'm not talking about bodies, men and women ... I refer to your nature and expression of personal masculine and feminine creative energy. Without understanding masculine and feminine energy, we can become very much out of balance. Have you ever noticed that the masculine and feminine don't quite communicate on the same wavelength? The masculine and feminine somehow seem to misconnect in this third dimensional reality. There is a very good reason for this ...

Using the concept of geometry, it is perhaps easier to understand that masculine energy is made up of straight lines and angles.

Feminine energy is made up of curves and swirls. There are no straight lines and angles in feminine energy just as there are no curves and swirls in masculine energy. Feminine energy is also very energized and fast. Masculine energy is slow and dull.

Feminine energy is very expansive, very creative, and very fluid. Feminine energy can do a dozen things at one time while it swirls and curves. Masculine energy says go down a straight line: go from point A to point B to point C and back to point A. Patrick Wanis, a Human Behaviorist added:

> If anything, I would, as a male, argue that the female energy is so much more powerful than the male energy for two key reasons: first and foremost, because the female energy is a reproductive energy; and second, because the female energy has so much power over the masculine. Women have a lot more power than men than they choose to understand, accept or embrace. Masculine energy is directive energy. It has a goal, it's focused, and it's about achievement or doing something. Femininity, on the other hand, is about receptive energy. It's about receiving, it's about being open.
>
> Interestingly, if you take a look at even the human body when comparing the male body with the female body, what you notice is that the male, even with his genitalia, can easily be described as directive energy. The female genitalia is receptive energy in the sense if you look at the male genitalia and how it connects and how the male and female connect when in intercourse, there's the directive energy, the male, there's the receptive — well, I said energy but really the directive — what's the correct word — the directive approach by the male and the receptive approach by the female body.

Nevertheless, as experienced magical practitioners are aware, a huge part of sex magic is about avoiding sex. Yep, that's right. Sex magic is not about having sex all the time, although there is a time and a place for that sort of approach. In order to receive maximum benefits of sex magic, the point is to *control* energy and manipulating energy is the key; while the power unleashed during the rite will be double, even triple, because of self-control. This is trusting in the Universe and let the Divine take over. By concentrating that energy then channeling it into our heart's desire, our wish becomes more potent. The best sex magic is one that starts with a cosmic whisper and bursts out with a rebel yell!

Magical Exercise

Donald Michael Kraig, the occultist and author of Modern Sex Magick back in 1998 made a valid comment:

I found many of the books on sex magick to be sexist: the man does this and the woman helps. Then the man does this and the woman helps. Then the man does something else and the woman helps. If you find a person who claims to know sex magick and is willing to teach you, I do not think that the first thing you should do is take off your clothes and start having sex. Rather, a legitimate teacher would give you concepts to study and do some energy work with you. When that is successful, you might move on to other techniques. It might take some time before anything an outsider might consider sexual activity would actually happen.

Aymen Fares, an Australian life-coach also shared some basic techniques of sex magick on his website (https://spiritual.com.au) based on the teachings of Aleister Crowley in regard to this fascinating subject. Crowley added a 'k' to the word 'magic' because this was the initial letter of the Greek *ktéis* (vagina), and this altered spelling symbolized the importance of sex in operative magic.

Solo Sex Magick based on the 'Crowley' O∴T∴O VIII degree. Formulate your purpose, put it on the back-burner and begin sexual stimulation. At orgasm:

- Males – your purpose should overwhelm your mind; your semen can either be consumed or used to charge a prepared talisman – needless to say the talisman should also express your purpose.

- Females – with each orgasm your purpose should overwhelm your mind; as the orgasm recedes put it to the background of your mind again – repeat until done. Your vaginal fluids can be treated in the same fashion as for the semen above.

This technique is particularly well adapted to the creation of 'magickal children' which are spirits dedicated to a specific purpose. In fact, some mystical groups believe that every time you masturbate you create a spirit, which is probably the religious basis for 'Do not masturbate'.

Heterosexual Sex Magick based on the 'Crowley' O∴T∴O IX degree. First of all, it's possible for one participant to do this with the other completely unaware of what is going on. Of course, there is a wealth of opinion on this – is it morally/ethically right or wrong? From a strictly practical viewpoint it's all or nothing. If you are going to use another person to do something like this then it will work best if they are either completely ignorant of what you are doing or completely on board – meaning a willing, knowledgeable and experienced participant. Partial awareness could adversely affect the performance or the result of the work. Under the assumption that both participants – male and the female are conscious of the working:

- The purpose should be agreed upon beforehand, concentrated upon, and back-grounded by both participants.

- The male participant's orgasm should be delayed as long as possible.
- Multiple orgasms in the female participant are desirable.
- Same rules apply at orgasm as for solo sex magick.
- After the male participant ejaculates, the mixed fluids are taken up by him via cunnilingus and shared with the female participant in a kiss.
- This elixir is then consumed.
- The elixir can also be used to charge a Talisman

There are slightly different formulae employed depending on whether the female participant is menstruating or not. (see Chapter Two)

Homosexual Sex Magick

Crowley also developed several formulae for homosexual sex magick which is the O∴T∴O XI degree. There is debate on whether this O∴T∴O degree actually means 'homosexual sex magick' or whether Crowley meant it to be, *'whatever you have the most personal inhibitions built up against'* and therefore this would charge your arousal to a higher state and give the work more power. Aymen Fares' personal opinion is that he meant the latter.

The main reason that the techniques of sex magick will not work for the majority of people who try it – is that they will not be clear enough in mind and emotion to set the correct wheels in motion. Most people have thoughts that are scattered and unfocused the vast majority of the time, let alone during sex. Further to that, they have so many thoughts that they are unaware of what they are actually thinking and the direction their mind is taking. Most people's emotional makeup will block the results of what they are trying to attain, especially if they have inadequate magical training/understanding of what they are trying to achieve.

Nevertheless, to say Aleister Crowley's writing is very much an acquired taste and, as a result, many contemporary witches dismiss much of his work. *'It veered on the more racist and sexist and just really weird,'* commented one. *'I feel that a lot of his work, for what it was, was very self-serving and low vibrational, very demonic in a sense where you're working with things that if you have no idea what the hell you're doing, you could fuck yourself up. I've never felt compelled to go any further with studying him.'*

Once he grasped the fundamentals of sexual magick, however, Aleister Crowley understood it to be the key that unlocks the secrets of the universe and he dedicated the entire second half of his life to exploring its mysteries. According to Sarane Alexandrian, he remains incontestably the pre-eminent master of 20th-century High Sexual Magic (which AC called the High Magick Art) Although Alexandrian observed: *'Despite all the reservations one may have regarding Crowley's exceptional temperament, the fact remains that his concept of sex as a magical key to the visible and invisible world is unique...'* It's obvious from his comments that he had trouble coming to grips with the Old Man's writing style!

Chapter Five

The Goddess as Cougar

In 21st century parlance, a 'cougar' is typically defined as an older woman who is primarily attracted to and may have a sexual relationship with significantly younger men. Although some consider 'cougar' a sexist, derogatory term, the flavor of the meaning in context varies from empowering to offensive since the meaning of the term seems to vary with the speaker. By contrast, within the modern witchcraft tradition, it is not unusual for younger men to be attracted to older women, and those with any understanding of the sexual dynamics within Craft are not surprised or upset by it.

To outsiders, however, the popular stereotype is of a heterosexual unmarried, middle-aged woman who maintains a youthful physical appearance, either by exercise, cosmetics, cosmetic surgery, or a combination of these. She is financially independent, and expresses her sexuality by publicly pursuing younger men for casual relationships or sexual encounters. She does so because she wants a partner who both appreciates and can satisfy a sexually assertive and self-sufficient woman. That stereotype also suggests that cougars are commonly looking for fun in their temporary sexual liaisons. At the same time, they are perceived as women who strive to correspond to strict, ageist conceptions of female beauty, i.e. maintaining a youthful appearance and slimness well into middle age.

And yet ... it was a common theme in ancient times when the older goddesses were paired with younger, virile youths. Goddesses symbolised the land. As ancient as the landscape, they were imagined as being restored to youth and fertility when united with a succession of younger, often mortal mates. Did these mythical and legendary women and men share qualities with the living women and men of the time? Were they admired? Were they seen as role models? Or were they seen as 'foolish and excessive' as some modern scholars think? In fact, in some cases the goddess of sexuality is seen as an old woman and Celtic folklore is replete with sexually active older goddesses, like Achtland and the over-eager Mal, who died pursuing a much younger man along the Irish coast.

But it's the cougars from Classical antiquity who have stood the test of time. Like Cybele and Attis - the story of the buxom Phrygian primal goddess's tragic love for the boyish god of vegetation who became her consort. As punishment for his infidelity, the goddess drove him into a mad frenzy which caused him to castrate himself; Initiates into the eunuch-priesthood of Cybele, known as *Gallai*, re-enacted this myth with an act of self-mutilation. This Phrygian cult was adopted and adapted by Greek colonists of Asia Minor, spreading to mainland Greece and later to Rome.

Artemis was the Olympian goddess of hunting, the wilderness and wild animals. The handsome hunter Orion was a companion of the goddess and much loved by her, but her jealous brother Apollo tricked her into killing him with a distant bow-shot. In her grief Artemis placed him amongst the stars as the constellation Orion. She was later identified as the patron of childbirth and protector of young girls, although her chastity might account for her waspishness. In general, however, the virginal interpretation of Artemis presided and she was believed to expect her priests and priestesses to live pure and chaste lives as well. Severe punishments were inflicted if one of her followers broke their vows of abstinence.

Aphrodite was the Olympian goddess of love, beauty and pleasure and procreation, depicted as a beautiful woman often accompanied by the winged godlet Eros (Love). Adonis was a youth of remarkable beauty and the mortal lover of the goddess. While Adonis was still in the first flush of youth and because of Artemis' or Ares' anger he was wounded by a boar during a hunt and died. The 19th-century anthropologist Sir James Frazer wrote extensively about Adonis in his monumental study of comparative religion *The Golden Bough,* in which he claimed that Adonis was just one example of the archetypical 'dying-and-rising god' found throughout all cultures. The entire story of Venus and Adonis originates in Roman mythology with the myth appearing in Book Ten of Ovid's *Metamorphoses;* a later *Venus and Adonis* was written early in Shakespeare's career and draws on the vogue of Ovidian and erotic poetry of the 1580s and 1590s.

And finally, among the gods of Babylonia none achieved wider and more enduring fame than Tammuz, who was loved by Ishtar, the amorous Queen of Heaven - the beautiful youth who died and was mourned for and came to life again does not figure by his popular name in any of the city pantheons, but from the earliest times until the passing of Babylonian civilization, he played a prominent part in the religious life of the people. Tammuz, is an ancient Mesopotamian god associated with shepherds, who was also the primary consort of the goddess Inanna (later known as Ishtar) goddess of war and sexual love. The cult of Inanna-Ishtar also heavily influenced the cult of the Phoenician goddess Astoreth, representing the productive power of nature and embodying the powers for new life in nature in the spring.

A 'cougar' can present both positive and negative images: They are independent, sexually confident women, or they are women striving to conform to the social norms of youth and beauty. The term 'cougar' is also an example of how modern culture defines and prescribes roles for (heterosexual) women and men (sugar daddy is a rich older man who lavishes gifts on a young woman in return for her company and/or sexual favours) in society. What these two have in common - aside from an age difference - is an imbalance of power and wealth, with the wealth and power being held primarily by the older person. The earliest documented use for the term 'cougar' as it pertains to a woman seeking such a relationship is said to have been in professional sports locker-room talk. In the 1980s, the Canadian ice hockey team the Vancouver Canucks used the term to refer to the older, single women who attended their hockey games to pursue players sexually.

Sociologist Milaine Alarie compiled statistics for her 2018 doctorate thesis on the subject of relationships defined by older women and younger men. She found that overall, and just as in the past, women typically marry men who are slightly older than they are. Alarie proposes that negative reactions to cougar relationships are so strong because they violate long-standing social norms. For example, there is an assumption in Western culture that men value youth and beauty in a partner, while women value financial stability. Men are also believed to have stronger sex drives than women and are expected to make the first contact, while women are encouraged to wait passively for men to choose them. Finally, there's the idea that older women are expected to be asexual. Cougar behavior turns all of these norms on their heads.

The meaning of the term 'cougar' seems to vary with the commentator. On the positive side, cougars are associated with gender equality, an outgrowth of the sexual revolution, and the availability of reliable contraceptives, which have given women more freedom when choosing a partner. They are also an explicit reflection that sexuality is not necessarily connected with childbearing. Moreover, an increase in status, education, and income means that a woman can establish herself as the more powerful party in a relationship (should an unequal power dynamic be desired by both partners).

However, there is a considerable negative undertone prevalent in the media, where cougars are often described as *'desperately aggressive'* or *'desperately clinging to youth'*. Surveys show that women generally feel that such behavior is ultimately dangerous for the men, themselves, or both. Cougars are seen as predators of unwary men or victims of the cultural imperative to find value in their physical appearance. But the drawbacks are severe: There is a social stigma, and men are often pressured by their friends and family to find someone younger. In a cougar relationship, women are not likely to want (more) children when their partner does, and while many men say that their partner's higher income is a benefit, some research shows that can also lead to conflict.

On the other side of the coin, Sugar Daddies and Sugar Babes have been around for centuries. *'There are evolutionary explanations behind the Sugar relationship phenomena'*, says Danielle in her *Let's Talk Sugar* Blog:

> *Men prefer younger, attractive women because they are more fertile. Women prefer older, successful men because they can provide for their offspring. The most famous early examples of Sugar Babies, however, were royal mistresses. These women were financially supported (often with a yearly allowance) by Kings. However, they were also often smart about it. They used the money and connections to secure a future for themselves rather than buying frivolous things.*

These included Diane de Poitiers, the chief mistress of King Henry II in the early 1500s who went on to become an influential member of the French court. In the 1600s, Nell Gwyn was kept by King Charles II of England and Scotland. She represented the classic Cinderella story of a poor actress becoming wealthy and powerful – and the ancestress of the Dukes of St Albans.

While in the 1700s, Madame de Pompadour was the official mistress of Louis XV who went on to become a powerful member of the court and secured noble titles for herself and her family.

These early cases paved the way for future Sugar relationships, although the first use of the term 'Sugar Daddy' didn't appear until the early 1900s when Adolph Spreckels, heir to a Sugar fortune, was *affectionately* referred to as a Sugar Daddy by his young wife Alma who was 24 years younger than him. By 1926, 'Sugar Daddy' had become a well-known slang term for a man who spoils a younger female companion with gifts or money. The Sugar lifestyle grew in popularity due to the 'flapper girl' culture of the Roaring Twenties.

By the 1950s, the idea had hit Hollywood with several popular movies based on the idea. Gentlemen Prefer Blondes and How to Marry a Millionaire both came out in 1953 featuring beautiful, young women (both films starred Marilyn Monroe) in pursuit of wealthy benefactors. Breakfast at Tiffany's came out in 1961 and quickly became a favorite of women everywhere. Since the film is vague, the Holly Golightly character is often thought of as an escort. Truman Capote himself saw the character as more of a kept woman. Unlike the women of the 20th century, the modern Sugar Baby takes a cue from the influential Sugar pioneers of the 1500s-1700s. She's more entrepreneurial. She is often looking for mentoring and help with tuition or student loans. Whereas in the past, an expensive beret and jewelry might have been enough. [Let's Talk Sugar]

So ... Is the cougar trend really anything new? This is not the first time in history that older women are dating younger men. This has been going on for centuries and Western culture has a well-documented case file. Take a look at the preferences of Queen Elizabeth I of England, Catherine the Great, Empress of Russia and Mae West; while French President Emmanuel Macron is married to Brigitte, 24 years his senior, who was a teacher at his high school. But once again, the sexual habits of women have captured media attention, and as a result yet another label is created to describe their behavior. So, is the older woman/younger man trend, really a trend?

In part, cougars produce uneasiness in people because of the moral ambiguity about aging and sexuality. On the positive side, cougars are associated with gender equality, an outgrowth of the sexual revolution. As Patti Somer writing in *303 Magazine* points out:

Older women are more confident and independent and don't need a man to 'complete' them. Been there, done that, and they're over it. They are realistic and mature, and because they are secure with themselves, they are less likely to become jealous, overly emotional, possessive, or obsessive, and they do not *have a ticking biological clock.*

A classy, older, worldly woman with a wealth of life experience can be intellectually stimulating as well as sexually stimulating. If she's lived life fully, she will have a treasure trove of interesting stories to share. She can teach you a thing or two about life, love, and women, and can also broaden your horizons in food, wine, travel, literature, film, and so forth.

According to William Langley, however, writing for the *Telegraph*, a recent scientific study warned that such females face a lower life expectancy. A German research organisation, the Max Planck Institute, claimed that women who took up with younger men were likely to have a much-reduced life expectancy. 'The best choice for a woman is to marry a man of exactly the same age,' said the institute's director, Sven Drefahl. '*The bigger the age gap, the greater the woman's chances of dying prematurely.*'

The even worse news was that men involved with younger women tended to live longer. So what's going on? The researchers suggested that women who take younger partners are seen to be 'violating social norms', and suffer ostracism from their families and neighbours to a degree that causes stress. The toll of it affects their health and morale, leading to increased mortality. Evolutionary psychology has long argued that the traditional protective role of the male predisposes women to take slightly older partners. Less prominently reported was evidence that women who marry significantly older men tend to die prematurely, too. Conclusion: a sugar daddy kills you just as surely as a toy-boy, so why not take the stud?

There was a time when any woman who looked much younger than her years was suspected of witchcraft, and even today mature witches are much more youthful than many people who are far younger than them. In keeping with the Tradition, younger men are attracted to older women who possess a greater depth of Craft knowledge and ability ... and they are relationships that have stood the test of time. Witches do tend to retain their vigour and perhaps it's not surprising that in the current climate of gender confusion, younger men are attracted to the mature witch who can help him improve his quality of life – and her witch-power gives an added appeal.

Magical Exercise

Another possibility suggested by Aymen Fares is visualising a god/goddess making love to us while we're masturbating. Gods and goddesses personify important human characteristics and talents/qualities, or aspects of life in their pure form. We can imagine ourselves in sexual union with a deity when we wish to strengthen or emphasise these qualities in ourselves.

We may need help for a specific goal, for instance from a goddess of love, a god of healing or a god specialised in divination. If this is the case, we start the ritual, by arousing ourselves and invoke the chosen god/goddess. Visualise the deity as vivid as we can with all our senses! Keep on repeating the name of the deity; and at the moment of orgasm we channel the energy into our goal (something related to the deity).

We may wish the god's help to improve certain qualities in ourselves: let's say intuition. In this case our goal is projected inside ourselves: while astrally making love, we absorb the divine energy which will help us manifest that same energy ourselves. Build up as much energy as we can before climaxing.

Thank and release the deity before we end the ritual! Working with a god/goddess can be intensely erotic because deities are free from negative sexual conditioning, they have no hang-ups, and bring along a great deal of energy. Be aware, however, that each deity has its own personality and they will bring it with during their love play. Therefore, we must know whom we invite. *Working with deities is not something any genuine magical practitioner would advise for beginners.*

We can even go further by invoking a god/goddess into our own body. Here we deliberately surrender our ego and offer ourselves completely for a higher purpose. We can work this deep and intense sex magic as described above: and at the end thank and release the deity! *Again: this is not for beginners. And never, never invoke an entity lower than a god/goddess into your body!*

But as Sarane Alexandrian points out in *The Great Work of the Flesh*, many Americans and Europeans flatter themselves in thinking they are tantric yoga practitioners, but it they have not first converted to Hinduism, it is an idle boast. As the purpose of the practice is the identification of the couple with Shiva and Shakti it is therefore necessary to believe in this god and goddess; otherwise this act is only a parody of what its true disciples are doing.

This drawback does not exist in Taoist sexuality because the sexual act is not performed under the invocation of the Chinese deities but in accordance with the Tao, The Great Principle, which involves the balance of Yin and Yang. A Western Christian can, without feeling he has renounced his faith, indulge in Taoist sexuality as it involves putting cosmic forces into play and not submitting to the gods of a foreign pantheon.

Sexual magic is not a collection of superstitions to be regarded with amused skepticism; it is created out of religious beliefs that have been redirected from their source and concentrated on the physics of love. Furthermore, superstitions are only survivals in the Christian era of the sacred principles that paganism upheld in its pantheistic worship and to which all citizens were loyal in that earlier period. There is a particular sex magic associated with every religion ...

During these solitary sex-sessions it is not uncommon to have the feeling that we are being watched and this is a completely normal phenomenon. When we are aroused it's possible that we open up psychic portals and this depends on who we are, what our current emotional state is, and many other factors that are pertinent to us as an individual. Whenever we practice magic, we automatically transmit an astral beacon that will attract all sorts of entities which is why it is essential that all our protections are in place by surrounding ourselves by a protective Circle.

The simplest and most powerful form of protection is casting the Invoking and Banishing Pentagram at the start and at the end of any ritual. We make the sign of the Invoking Pentagram by raising our right thumb nail to our forehead then moving our hand down to the middle of our left thigh; up to our right shoulder then across to the left shoulder; down to our right thigh and back up to our forehead – thus completing the pentagram to begin the rite. When tracing the pentagram do make it large even if performing solitary.

The Banishing Pentagram is made in reverse by moving our right hand down to the middle of our left thigh; up to our forehead and from there moving the hand down to the middle of the right thigh; then upwards to the left shoulder, straight over to the right shoulder and return to the starting point of the left thigh. The Pentagram ritual may, incidentally, be used as a form of prayer by using the Invoking Pentagram in the morning and the Banishing Pentagram in the evening.

Here ... at the End of All Things

Hopefully, it is understood that sex magic is *not* about clambering into the Circle for a quick shag because during initial training there is often no physical contact at all. Here we are talking about harnessing the masculine and feminine energies that reside in all of us regardless of gender. In *Coven Working*, the authors explained that they had operated successful teaching groups for many years that included men and women of all sexual persuasions without exclusion or bias. During that time, they had, of course, encountered problems and prejudices on *both* sides of the 'gay divide' and would say right from the start, that the refusal to welcome gays into a predominantly straight group says more about the coven leader's *personal* prejudices than it does about their magical teaching capabilities. The West-Wright duo admit there *are* a number of difficulties and misunderstandings that can and do arise with regard to gay and lesbian approaches to magical practice within Craft, but they refute those who claim (quite wrongly) that gays have no place in a modern straight coven.

With this understanding about magic, we realize that we are absolutely free to do whatever we want to do while being responsible for our own actions. When we embrace this freedom, religious and social leaders can no longer have power over us. When we step outside the bounds of sexual behaviour many social gurus want to impose, we increase our level of freedom said Donald Michael Kraig, author of *Modern Sex Magick* said to *Tryangle* magazine:

> But while sex magic is popular among witches now, it also has ancient roots. In the earliest days, it was clear that sexual practices and sex magic were far more widespread and accepted than they are today. This is evidenced in historical records of pagan cultures

and even into ancient Greece and Rome. There are records of such practices found in ancient India and China. As societies grew, people hungry for power and control over others condemned sex and magic. As a result, the practices went underground. Sex, magic, and sex-magic were at one time practiced by many, if not most people. The practices were not special; they were just what people did. Over time, narrow-minded social and religious leaders had sex, magic, and sex-magic practices not merely condemned, but outlawed ... and still they survived.

In many instances the battle of the sexes has become the division of the sexes as a result of MeToo in the workplace. A report in the *Harvard Business Review* stated that:

Men would be more apt to exclude women from social interactions, such as after-work drinks ... 19% of men said they were reluctant to hire attractive women, 21% said they were reluctant to hire women for jobs involving close interpersonal interactions with men (jobs involving travel, say), and 27% said they avoided one-on-one meetings with female colleagues; "I'm not sure we were surprised by the numbers, but we were disappointed," says Rachel Sturm, a professor at Wright State University who worked on the project. "When men say, 'I'm not going to hire you, I'm not going to send you traveling, I'm going to exclude you from outings' — those are steps backward.

All this talk of harassment is very difficult for *everyone* because nobody even knows what sexual harassment is anymore! If we observe the behavior of men together after work, in the pub, or at the gym – which can probably be described as intimate but certainly not sexy – if a man were to behave in *exactly* the same way toward a woman, she'd be screaming 'sexual harassment' in less time than it takes for Dolly Parton to belt out *Nine to Five*!

At one stage most women were perfectly aware of the

difference between a friendly hug and a creepy hug in the workplace. The trouble was that *male* onlookers didn't realize that Dave got away with it because his manner was friendly, neither sexual nor threatening; when Gerald tried the same thing and got reported for harassment, it could perhaps be understood why he became angry and didn't understand he was classed as 'creepy'. It's now got to the stage where men are afraid to even shake a woman's hand in case she thinks it's harassment! Easier to just avoid contact altogether! And ironically, reports show that women employers are also becoming more wary about taking on women ...

Those coming to the Coven for instruction are kept in relative isolation while they complete the foundation course, because we wouldn't have them in the Coven if we thought their presence was going to cause trouble. One of our witches had problems with her former coven when the Lady felt the Man in Black was taking too much of an interest in the attractive, blonde professional dancer. The story got around and she was welcomed into her present coven – perhaps because the new Dame and Magister were more secure in their relationship and although there's a lot of sexist teasing goes on, no one is offended or threatened by it.

Fortunately, the Coven can still joke about the conflict between male and female gender roles as being a blue or pink job when it comes to leading the seasonal rituals in the Circle, for example. 'Conducting the Candlemas ritual is a pink job', or 'Taking charge of the Stang is a blue job'. And refer to something being 'a man thing' or 'women's logic' during magical discussions when the question is raised that some of the others can't follow, or agree with ... such as why the chaps would rather turn blue and not admit to freezing due to the lack of layers underneath their robe; while our ladies will be cozily tucked up into thermals and fleeces under theirs? Humour of a non-malicious variety can cross many boundaries ... because since when did the question of whom we sleep with become such an ill-tempered and humourless battle-zone.

Masculine and feminine energies power *all* magic in the Circle regardless of gender, and usually without manifesting in any form of sexual activity. And because we are taught to restore the harmony between gender and sex within Old Craft practice with our understanding of the flexibility and fluidity of the two, we all – men and women - learn to move beyond stereotypical gender roles in Circle. Outside the Circle, women by their own machinations seem to be excluding themselves from social contact with men but personally, I think most Old Crafters would still rather be thought of as just one of the girls and boys!

Sources & Bibliography

The Arte of Darkness, Mélusine Draco (Ignotus)

Coven Working, Carrie West and Philip Wright (Ignotus)

The Equinox Vol III, No I, Aleister Crowley (Weiser)

The Great Work of the Flesh, Sarene Alexandrian (Desiny) (Destiny)

Magic in the Middle Ages, Richard Kieckhefer (CUP)

Malleus Satani, Suzanne Ruthven (Ignotus)

Pan: Dark Lord of the Forest and Horned Gods of the Witches, Mélusine Draco (Moon Books)

Paschal Beverly Randolph, John Patrick Deveney (SUNY)

Seeking the Primal Goddess, Mélusine Draco (Moon Books)

Sex, Dissidence and Damnation, Jeffery Richards (Routledge)

Sex Magic for Beginners, Skye Alexander (Llewellyn)

Sexual Outlaw, Erotic Mystic: The Essential Ida Craddock, Vere Chappell (Weiser)

Sexuality in Medieval Europe, Ruth Mazzo Karras (Routledge)

The Thelemic Handbook, Mélusine Draco (Ignotus)

Internet Sources

https://www.theoi.com/

https://www.patheos.com/blogs/thewitchesnextdoor/

https://www.theguardian.com/news/2018/may/11/how-metoo-revealed-the-central-rift-within-feminism-social-individualist

https://spiritual.com.au/2011/07/sex-magick-rituals/

https://www.spiralnature.com/reviews/great-work-of-the-flesh-alexandrian/

About the Author

Mélusine Draco, as her name suggests, has long been plugged into the powerful currents of traditional witchcraft and ritual magic. She is one of the real ones. Her provocative writing will show you how to move between the inner and outer worlds. Follow along behind her if you dare.

Alan Richardson, author of numerous esoteric titles including *Priestess* and *The Old Sod*, biographies of Dion Fortune and W G Gray.

Mélusine Draco is an Initiate of traditional British Old Craft and the Khemetic Mysteries. Her highly individualistic teaching methods and writing draw on historical sources supported by academic texts and current archaeological findings; endorsing Crowley's view that magic(k) is an amalgam of science and art, and that magic is the outer route to the inner Mysteries. Author of over fifty titles, many currently published with John Hunt Publishing including the best-selling six-part Traditional Witchcraft series; *Power of the Elements, By Spellbook & Candle; The Dictionary of Magic & Mystery, Magic Crystals, Sacred Stones* and *The Atum-Re Revival*. Her esoteric novels in the Temple House Archive series are available in both paperback and e-book formats – all books are available on Amazon.

Other Mélusine Draco titles published by Moon Books

Traditional Witchcraft for Urban Living
Traditional Witchcraft for the Seashore
Traditional Witchcraft for the Fields & Hedgerows
Traditional Witchcraft for the Woods & Forests
Traditional Witchcraft and the Pagan Revival
Traditional Witchcraft and the Path to the Mysteries
The Dictionary of Magic & Mystery
Black Horse, White Horse: Equine Magical Lore
Aubrey's Dog: Canine Magical Lore
Magic Crystals, Sacred Stones
The Atum-Re Revival
By Spellbook and Candle: Cursing, Hexing, Bottling & Binding
The Coarse Witchcraft Trilogy (ghost written and edited)
The Secret People: Parish-pump witchcraft,
Wise-women and Cunning Ways
Pan: Dark Lord of the Forest and Horned God of the Witches
By Wolfsbane & Mandrake Root: The Shadow World of Plants and
Their Poisons
Having A Cool Yule: How To Survive (and Enjoy) the Mid-Winter
Festival)
Divination: By Rod, Birds and Fingers
The Power of the Elements
Seeking the Primal Goddess
The (Inner-City) Path
Sacred Landscape: Caves & Mountains

Web: www.covenofthescales.com and www.templeofkhem.com
Blog: https://wordpress.com/view/Mélusine-draco.blog

**MOON
BOOKS**

PAGANISM & SHAMANISM

What is Paganism? A religion, a spirituality, an alternative belief
system, nature worship? You can find support for all these defini-
tions (and many more) in dictionaries, encyclopaedias, and text
books of religion, but subscribe to any one and the truth will evade
you. Above all Paganism is a creative pursuit, an encounter with
reality, an exploration of meaning and an expression of the soul.
Druids, Heathens, Wiccans and others, all contribute their insights
and literary riches to the Pagan tradition. Moon Books invites you
to begin or to deepen your own encounter, right here, right now.
If you have enjoyed this book, why not tell other readers by
posting a review on your preferred book site.

Recent bestsellers from Moon Books are:

Journey to the Dark Goddess
How to Return to Your Soul
Jane Meredith
Discover the powerful secrets of the Dark Goddess and
transform your depression, grief and pain into healing
and integration.
Paperback: 978-1-84694-677-6 ebook: 978-1-78099-223-5

Shamanic Reiki
Expanded Ways of Working with Universal Life Force Energy
Llyn Roberts, Robert Levy
Shamanism and Reiki are each powerful ways of healing; together,
their power multiplies. *Shamanic Reiki* introduces techniques to
help healers and Reiki practitioners tap ancient healing wisdom.
Paperback: 978-1-84694-037-8 ebook: 978-1-84694-650-9

Pagan Portals – The Awen Alone
Walking the Path of the Solitary Druid
Joanna van der Hoeven
An introductory guide for the solitary Druid, *The Awen Alone* will
accompany you as you explore, and seek out your own place
within the natural world.
Paperback: 978-1-78279-547-6 ebook: 978-1-78279-546-9

A Kitchen Witch's World of Magical Herbs & Plants
Rachel Patterson
A journey into the magical world of herbs and plants, filled with
magical uses, folklore, history and practical magic. By popular
writer, blogger and kitchen witch, Tansy Firedragon.
Paperback: 978-1-78279-621-3 ebook: 978-1-78279-620-6

Medicine for the Soul

The Complete Book of Shamanic Healing

Ross Heaven

All you will ever need to know about shamanic healing and how to become your own shaman...

Paperback: 978-1-78099-419-2 ebook: 978-1-78099-420-8

Shaman Pathways – The Druid Shaman

Exploring the Celtic Otherworld

Danu Forest

A practical guide to Celtic shamanism with exercises and techniques as well as traditional lore for exploring the Celtic Otherworld.

Paperback: 978-1-78099-615-8 ebook: 978-1-78099-616-5

Traditional Witchcraft for the Woods and Forests

A Witch's Guide to the Woodland with Guided Meditations and Pathworking

Mélusine Draco

A Witch's guide to walking alone in the woods, with guided meditations and pathworking.

Paperback: 978-1-84694-803-9 ebook: 978-1-84694-804-6

Naming the Goddess

Trevor Greenfield

Naming the Goddess is written by over eighty adherents and scholars of Goddess and Goddess Spirituality.

Paperback: 978-1-78279-476-9 ebook: 978-1-78279-475-2

Shapeshifting into Higher Consciousness
Heal and Transform Yourself and Our World with Ancient
Shamanic and Modern Methods
Llyn Roberts
Ancient and modern methods that you can use every day to
transform yourself and make a positive difference in the world.
Paperback: 978-1-84694-843-5 ebook: 978-1-84694-844-2

Readers of ebooks can buy or view any of these bestsellers by
clicking on the live link in the title. Most titles are published in
paperback and as an ebook. Paperbacks are available in traditional
bookshops. Both print and ebook formats are available online.

Find more titles and sign up to our readers' newsletter at
http://www.johnhuntpublishing.com/paganism
Follow us on Facebook at https://www.facebook.com/MoonBooks
and Twitter at https://twitter.com/MoonBooksJHP